Copyright © 2016 by Matthew Lenza, Esq.

All rights reserved. No part of this publication may be reproduced, distributed, or transmitted in any form or by any means, including photocopying, recording, or other electronic or mechanical methods, without the prior written permission of the below named, except in the case of brief quotations embodied in critical reviews and certain other noncommercial uses permitted by copyright law. For permission requests, write to the below, addressed "Attention: Permissions Coordinator," at the address below.

Matthew Lenza, Esq.
c/o Lenza Law Firm, PLLC
1110 South Avenue
Staten Island, New York 10314

Legal Disclaimer: This book contains the opinions and ideas of the author. It is intended to provide an overview of some very complicated topics. It is sold with the sole understanding that the author is not engaged in rendering any services to any reader of this book. If any reader shall require further clarification, wish to engage in further discussion, or require personal advice, it is suggested that a competent professional representative be consulted. The author and publisher specifically disclaim any responsibility for any loss, risk or liability, personal or otherwise which results from any reliance or use of any information contained herein.

Ordering Information:

Quantity sales. Special discounts are available on quantity purchases by corporations, associations, and others. For details, contact the publisher at the address above.

Acknowledgements

"Family is not an important thing. It's everything."

-Michael J. Fox

I would like to thank some very important people for their support in getting this book published.

Thank you to my wife Erica, who *always* has and always will support any idea that I come up with and who has taught me the real meaning of unconditional love. Thank you to my mother, Josette, who taught me that the true measure of a person is their ability to always do the right thing. Thank you to my grandparents, who taught me about compassion for others and gave me the ability to see the good inside of everyone. Thank you to Maria and Enrique, who have embraced me as a son. Thank you to Mona, my editor, who was an invaluable part of getting this information from my mind onto these pages. Lastly, thank you to all of the colleagues and support staff that I have worked with through the years. I firmly believe that nobody can ever achieve true professional success without a strong foundation to rely on, and I owe each of you a great gratitude.

Table of Contents

Foreword...	i
Chapter 1- When The Unthinkable Happens.........................	1
Chapter 2- Do I Need An Attorney?...................................	4
Chapter 3- Wills And Trusts..	11
Chapter 4- Planning For Incapacity....................................	33
Chapter 5- Who Will Care For Your Children?.......................	41
Chapter 6- How To Leave Property And Money To Your Children	46
Chapter 7- Planning For Special Needs Children.....................	51
Chapter 8- What About Life Insurance?...............................	58
Chapter 9- Dealing With Retirement Plans In The Context Of An Estate Plan	66
Chapter 10- Prenuptial and Postnuptial Agreements.................	78
Chapter 11- Handling Estate Planning Issues After A Divorce....	88
Chapter 12- Estate Taxes and Gift Taxes.............................	96
Chapter 13- Estate Planning for Unmarried Couples................	112

Chapter 14- Married and Unmarried Couples - Jointly Held Property   118

Chapter 15- Social Media Accounts and Digital Assets.............   124

Chapter 16- Pets and Pet Trusts..   131

Chapter 17- Estate Planning for the Same-Sex Couple.............   136

Chapter 18- Legacy Planning...   141

Chapter 19- Estate Planning for Family Business Owners.........   145

Chapter 20- Making Changes: How Your Estate Plan Should Evolve   151

Chapter 21- Advanced Planning Techniques........................   157

Chapter 22- How To Select An Estate Planning Attorney.........   165

Conclusion- Summing it all up...   172

Appendix...   174

Estate Planning For Young Families

What you NEED to know!

Foreword

So you finished school, started working full time and decided to start a family. The American Dream is yours. You have put down your roots and now you are ready to sit back and enjoy spending time and growing old with your family. As a parent, it may be an awful challenge to plan for the possibility that you may not see your children grow up. But, it's an important responsibility. If you avoid thinking about it, you risk leaving important decisions about the care of your children in the hands of others. By purchasing this book, you have taken an important first step; it proves that you are at least mindful of some important and often uncomfortable issues.

This book was drafted to **provide you with information** that will help you understand how to best provide for and protect your children should you and /or your significant other ever be unable to do so. In this book you will find discussions about how to plan for your own death or incapacitation and also how to plan for the death or incapacitation of a loved one. This is an important concept to understand before reading any further. The information contained in this book has been carefully curated. The contents are based on real-life client consultations, with often-asked questions and their corresponding answers. This book was not written to "get you into an attorney's office" for a consultation.

Many of you will read the information presented here and not immediately contact an attorney to discuss estate planning. That is not only expected but in some circumstances it is encouraged. It takes a certain emotional strength to even consider some of the issues necessary in preparing an estate plan. Only once you feel comfortable discussing these tough issues is it appropriate to move forward to the next step. I do recommend, however, that you speak with your significant other* sooner rather than later. The whole point of an estate plan designed for a younger family is to do some planning NOW, to save time, stress and money later.

Even if this book doesn't motivate you to immediately initiate any estate planning, it will help you understand the options available and open up a dialogue. That is one of my goals.

Our minds are occupied every day by things that we consider important. Perhaps a car needs repair, a child is suffering from a terrible cold, you have an important deadline at work, or your favorite TV show has been cancelled. I'm not going to tell you that any of those things aren't "important," because in the context of that day they probably are. Estate

*The term "significant other" is used for ease of communicating terms of wife, husband, boyfriend, girlfriend, partner, etc.

planning stands on a different level of importance; something that I like to term "life important." Your car will get fixed. Heck you will probably have 5 more in your life and you will fall in love with another TV show soon enough. "Life important" things have enormous consequences. The difference between proper estate planning and no planning is the tremendous effect that your actions or inactions will have on those you love. Your children will be directly affected by your disability or death. My work has made me witness to unfortunate situations where failure to plan has led to hundreds of thousands of dollars being taken from children, who would otherwise have been entitled to it if proper planning steps had been taken.

This book has been written with a specific intention to use as much plain language as possible. Any book written on legal matters will undoubtedly contain some confusing sections. As the title of the book states, this book is filled with information that you NEED to know! If you want to delve further into any specific area discussed here, I have included some helpful links in the appendix located at the end of the book and I urge you to visit those resources to broaden your knowledge of this sometimes-complex subject area.

One quick note about me before we get going. In my career as both an attorney and a professor at Saint John's University, I have done a lot of reading. One of my biggest pet peeves is when I am trying to learn something and the author or lecturer just gives broad sweeping information without really giving any specific or concrete direction. In my opinion, doing that is like trying to teach someone to swim by explaining to them the chemical composition of the ocean. This is why I have written this book with the thought of you, the reader, stepping into my office for a first consultation and without having done any prior research. Most of the chapters are fairly short and can easily be re-read if necessary to ensure that you have fully digested the information. As with any consultation, I will provide you the necessary information and then outline a plan. I hope you enjoy it.

Chapter 1

When the unthinkable happens

Consider this: You and your significant other are preparing for a rare weekend getaway to celebrate an anniversary. You have decided to go alone without your young children. To ensure that your children are safe and cared for while you are away, you dropped off your children with a trusted relative (Pro tip: Grandparents LOVE to watch Grandchildren!). You have carefully explained your children's needs, from the foods they eat to their usual bedtime routine. You reminded your relative of your childrens' allergies and their pediatrician's information. Lastly, you told your relative where you are going and how you can be reached in case something happens to your children while you are away. You are a great parent and when you leave those children to go out you really do feel that you are "covered." With so much preparation, you leave your children behind with the peace of mind that your children are well taken care of for the weekend.

What if you never made it back home?

Isn't it amazing that many parents never consider what preparations are in effect if you never return from the trip? I firmly believe that such thinking is often against human nature. For some reason, our minds are inherently trained since birth to focus on immediate consequences before considering those that will affect us in the long term. Doesn't it seem strange that we take so much care in our plans to be away for a weekend yet leave no instructions for the care of our children in the event that we never return? Just as providing instructions to your babysitting relative will give you peace of mind during your weekend away, planning for the security of your children in the event of your death will give you peace of mind **every day**. This is why I believe that every person with a partner and everyone with a young child needs to have an estate plan.

We don't get to choose when we pass on. What many fail to realize is that your estate plan is not planning for the estate that you have today, but for your estate as it will exist on that inevitable and often unexpected day when we all leave this world.

"But I don't have much of an estate." If this is what you are thinking, you are not alone. Estate planning doesn't mean you own "an estate," like an uber-wealthy person. It is all that you have – including your rights as a parent - and want to have distributed when you're not around to do it. You may even have estate items that you don't know you have. You might have a pension or other retirement plan or life insurance policy set up through your employer. Remember that a properly executed estate plan will survive and grow with you until your death. Thus, most young families need to plan for a much larger estate than they originally thought they had. People get raises, 401k accounts grow, stock portfolios expand, etc. To steal a quote from the great Ferris Bueller, "Life moves pretty fast."

Chapter 2

Do I need an attorney or can I just handle this on my own?

Now that you understand how important it is to make a plan, what do you need and how do you actually do it? This is a country founded on Yankee ingenuity and why would anyone want to pay someone to do something that they can do themselves? Why not save money to leave for the family instead of paying a lawyer? The Internet and office supply stores have the forms, so why not? Here's why not: LegalZoom, Quicken Will Forms and their myriad competitors are quite frankly much better at television and internet marketing than they are at understanding and utilizing estate planning concepts. By now you understand that I am an Estate Planning attorney and that my livelihood depends on whether people decide to use me to handle their Estate Planning needs. You likely expect me to simply downplay the DIY (Do-It-Yourself) Estate Planning services available because I have a vested financial interest in people not using these services. Nothing could be further from the truth. First of all, I'm only licensed in 2 of the 50 states of our fair country, so unless you live in New York or New Jersey, I legally cannot help you with your Estate Plan, even if you offered me five times my normal fee for preparing a plan. Second, I have gone to great lengths to fairly analyze the pros and cons of using an attorney to handle your Estate Planning needs versus using a DIY option. So, now I'll break it down for you.

If your only two choices are either doing no planning at all or downloading and executing forms from an online website or office supply store, use the forms.

I have reviewed tons of DIY forms, brought into my office by my clients. About half of the forms will work to accomplish *something* positive in terms of planning. For these clients, the sample forms work in *very limited circumstances*. The other 50% are absolutely useless. Here's what you need to know first: every State in the U.S. has its own rules about what happens to your assets and your rights when you die or become incapacitated (meaning, utterly unable to make your own decisions). Many DIY forms are drafted in a one-size-fits-all or a one-form-fits-all-states style. So, basically if your form doesn't have a section that is required in your state, the document could be completely worthless. The other problem is that these forms are drafted using confusing language and many are written in such poor English that the documents become truly worthless.

The major problem with using form documents is that "simple" documents do not necessarily achieve the result that is right for everyone. You are not a one-size-fits-all person and therefore, what is good planning for one person's estate is not necessarily good for you. Day after day, I see "simple" online or DIY documents that create a disaster and leave absolutely horrible situations for loved ones to clean up when you have passed. The unintended irony is that this is often worse than what you tried to prevent by preparing an estate plan in the first place. Because these documents are meant to help your loved ones carry out your wishes when you cannot do so yourself, you want to be sure that your instructions can be understood and implemented as smoothly as possible.

Remember, the document you execute is a legal document, which means that it's made to protect your interests in court. If it doesn't have what a court needs to see, it's just no good. It's not enforceable. And the company, which sold it to you is not legally responsible; read the fine print. When you die there is always a possibility that someone will challenge your estate documents in court. Part of my practice as an estate planning and elder law attorney is **probate litigation**. This means that I go to court to fight about someone's estate after they've died. As we become an increasingly litigious society, this reality is becoming more and more prevalent. The reality of estate litigation is that a professionally prepared estate plan is much less likely to be challenged, or to take it a step further *successfully* challenged, than an online or DIY estate plan. You want whatever document presented to a court to be enforceable – it must have force (not fluff).

So to extrapolate what was discussed above, here's a scenario to play out for clarification:

You are a smart, successful and prudent member of a young family living in California. You have decided (correctly) that you need to create an estate plan to prepare for all contingencies. In an effort to save money, you decide to utilize an online legal document service for a variety of estate planning documents. Tragically, one year after following the instructions to the letter on the downloaded documents, you are involved in a terrible automobile accident. Your significant other arrives at the hospital with your Health Care Directive document (discussed in later chapters) only to be told by the hospital staff that the document may not conform to the legal requirements in California, and they will not honor his or her wishes with respect to your treatment. The reason for this is because the hospital staff (petrified about being held liable to a different family member should they do *anything* against the letter of the law) refuses to acknowledge the document because it doesn't conform to California requirements. Who is your partner going to call from the hospital bedside, diy-estate-forms.com? I don't think they are going to have someone standing by to advocate on your behalf, if there is even someone available to discuss the matter with you at all. Having a trusted advisor to step in and straighten things out for you is worth much more than the few hundred dollars you will save by going it alone to begin with.

Continuing the hypothetical situation described above, you eventually succumb to your injuries, and your significant other now finds your Last Will and Testament (also discussed in a following chapter) and brings it to a local attorney so that the process of distributing your assets can begin to take place. Another family member, not satisfied with the "professionalism" of your Will document because it has not been prepared by an attorney, visits a separate attorney, who finds that the Will may not have been prepared according to all statutory requirements and that the Will may be invalid.

So let's now take stock of what has happened. You have had a horrifying experience in the last days of your life and what happens as a result may be in direct conflict with your stated wishes. Then, certain members of your family are now fighting over your estate, spending all kinds of time and money and destroying the fabric of a healthy family structure.

Do not kid yourself into thinking that this scenario is far-fetched or even unlikely. Because of what I do for a living, I promise you that variations of what I've just described happen every single day. It is heartbreaking to see a family torn apart over issues that could have been completely avoided with some properly completed basic estate planning. Let's discuss some of the tools that can be used to create a great estate plan for you and your family.

Chapter 3

Wills and Trusts

When I meet someone new and explain that I am an estate planning attorney, they often will ask me if that means that I handle "Wills and stuff." Wills and related document preparation are in fact a part of my practice. Another estate planning (and asset distribution) device, which winds up being much less expensive in the long run, is called a Trust.

What is a Will?

You likely already have a basic understanding of what a Last Will and Testament document is. In common parlance, most people just refer to it as a "Will." In short, a Will is a document that is prepared while someone is alive, which gives instructions as to how to distribute their property upon their death. Sometimes the Will instructions are very general, as when someone with adult children has a Will drafted that splits all of their assets equally among their children at the time of their death. Some people choose to specifically list all of their assets and make a specific determination as to whom they wish each asset or item will go to following their death. An example of this would be a clause in a Will that says that a diamond engagement ring should pass to a daughter, or treasured friend.

This sounds simple enough, right? Make a list of your assets, decide which specific items go to which specific person, and move on. **If only it were that simple! Between now and the time you die, many events can take place, which might make your Will decisions confusing after your death.** A simple (and common) example is the possibility of the person to whom you left an asset to dies before you. Estate planning is about foreseeing common possibilities and to consider the specific dynamics of each family.

There is no right answer regarding who should be the beneficiaries of an estate. The law is very clear that, other than disinheriting a spouse (which is impermissible to some extent in ALL states), you can leave some or all of your estate to anyone you like. You may bequeath your assets to a friend, uncle, nephew, cousin, or even a pet! The good news is that, when it comes to the distribution of **_YOUR_** estate, there IS a right answer. Your assets can pass to whomever **_YOU_** want and for whatever reasons you want.

Each State has its own requirements about how to properly create a Will. Most Wills need to be in writing, witnessed and involve the use of a notary public. Be wary though, as there are very specific little quirks that each state has when it comes to the drafting of Wills. Unfortunately, in Estate Planning there is really no such thing as "close enough" when determining whether a Will is valid or not. One simple error will invalidate the entire document and could (and does!) force the distribution of assets in a manner that will not comport with your wishes.

What is a Trust?

At some point in your life, you may have heard someone mention the use of a trust as an estate planning mechanism. Today, the use of Trusts has become a "go-to" estate planning tool for practitioners nationwide. This guide will provide you with all the information you need to understand Trusts. In this chapter I will explain what a Trust is, what it is used for, the types of Trusts available, and whether a young family should even be considering one. Your first question is likely quite simple- what exactly is a trust? Does it have to do with having faith in someone to do the right thing for you, as the colloquial use of the word trust might indicate? The answer to this is actually both yes and no.

I have taken much time in devising some basic analogies for my clients, which help to turn complex legal concepts into easily understandable ideas. My teaching work at Saint John's University has shown me that even students familiar with studying advanced legal concepts struggle with these premises. I will try explain to you what I teach my students, but you have the great luxury of not worrying about all of the case law to study and the exams to take.

Think of a Trust as a silent man who stands in the corner of a room. He is someone you TRUST. This man has two jobs in his life. First, he will hold anything that you give him, big or small (real estate, money, stock accounts, jewelry, etc.) for as long as you want him to hold it, even after you die. Second, he will distribute whatever he is holding for you according to a specific set of instructions that you have given him. Now imagine that instead of a person doing this for you, it's just an artificial entity, known as a Trust. There are two steps to the proper use of a Trust. First is the creation of the Trust and second is the funding of the Trust.

Creating a Trust

First, you must define the parameters of the Trust. This explains in a specific and personalized document exactly what your objectives are. A qualified estate planning attorney is the person who will discuss important life matters with you, ask you questions and draft the document for you. Important items to discuss include who you want to appoint to distribute (hand out) your assets upon your death (a "Trustee") and who will receive the assets of your Trust ("Beneficiaries") and in what percentages. There are different types of Trusts, which will be discussed later in this chapter. Once the document is completed the attorney should send you a copy for you to review and then answer any questions you have. Once you fully understand the documents, you will sign the document, typically in the attorney's office in the presence of two witnesses and a notary. These formal steps are known as the laws of document execution and must be followed exactly for the Trust to be valid and enforceable.

Funding a Trust

It is very important to note that a trust will only be useful to the extent that it has been funded. Remember the silent trusted man from the analogy above? You can hand him the most detailed list of how to distribute the things that he holds for you, but what if you never actually give him anything to hold? The Trust then becomes useless. From a practical perspective, this situation does occur more than you might think. The estate planning attorney's role in the creation of a trust is to draft a solid document that can accomplish the wishes of the person(s) for whom the trust is drafted. Only that person can take the equally important step (with guidance from their attorney) to fund the Trust and complete the work necessary to effectively utilize the benefits of the Trust.

The law permits estate planning professionals to get VERY creative with the drafting of trusts and the field of Trusts and Estates law is extremely confusing to the layperson and attorneys alike. The treatises written on this broad subject are voluminous. My purpose here is not to make you an expert on every type of Trust; that would be my job if a client would retain me as their attorney (and believe me, the cost for that is significantly higher than the price you paid for this book!). I simply want you to understand some basic concepts. You should absolutely explore advanced topics with your estate planning professional, should you wish to learn more about the subject. Before we begin the actual discussion of the different types of trusts, their benefits and restrictions, I want you to ask yourself the following two questions, which will help you to understand the differences in Trust options and WHY people use Trusts:

Question 1: Do I lose the ability to *control* or *remove* anything that I put into the trust?

Question 2: Do I gain any kind of *asset protection* benefit should I become sick, disabled, or need institutionalized care of some kind?

There are essentially three main parties involved in the creation of the trust.

1. The **Grantor** (a.k.a. the "Settlor"): The person who is creating the Trust and funding the Trust. Note that multiple people (e.g., a husband and a wife) can be the grantors on the same Trust.

2. The **Trustee**: The person designated to manage the assets placed within the Trust. Think of the trustee as the conductor of the trust (train

or orchestra - your choice!). The trustee directs the trust assets to where they need to go according to the wishes of the grantor.

3.   The **Beneficiary**: The person(s) who will receive the benefits or payout (money, property, etc.) of the Trust at a time or event certain (usually the death of the grantor).

Trust Type #1: Lifetime (Revocable) Trusts

The first type of trust is called a Lifetime (or Revocable) Trust. It's also commonly referred to as a Revocable Family Trust, Inter-Vivos Trust or a Living Trust. All four terms are pretty much synonymous in their practical use. Simply put, you place your assets into this Trust and use it for your own benefit during your lifetime. Upon your death, whatever remains in the Trust gets passed along to your pre-determined beneficiaries (e.g., your children). Typically, you would make yourself the original trustee of your lifetime trust, which would give you full ability to buy, sell, or give property or money in whatever quantity you see fit and however often you like. Even though the property is held in the name of the Trust, by naming yourself as a trustee, you retain the right to use it however and whenever you want and for any purpose. Most people find that there is absolutely no practical difference between managing money and property held in their own name versus managing the same items held in a Lifetime Revocable Trust. You still can get an ATM/Debit card and a checkbook to use the funds as you see fit. You also have the ability to name a successor trustee in the Trust document. This person would automatically take over the management of your affairs and distribution of your assets upon your disability or death.

In this type of Trust, you maintain the right to manage your property whether you're the trustee or not, since you have a right to change the terms of the Trust, the trustee, and the property in the trust at any time. When you die, your successor trustee distributes the property according to the terms of the Trust. Usually, your successor trustee will be your surviving spouse or an adult child, but many people name a bank or trust company instead (typically with a fee involved).

Living Trusts give you wide flexibility in distributing your property. For example, the Trust could say "at my death, my trustee is to give my car to my son, Robert; my boat to my daughter Jane;" and so on. Your instructions can tell the trustee to continue managing assets for the benefit of someone else, distribute them to any beneficiaries you choose, or perform some combination of these actions. If beneficiaries of your living trust die before you do, the property reverts to you, unless you've named other people (contingent beneficiaries) for those distributions.

There are some major benefits involved in using a Lifetime Revocable Trust to manage your assets during your lifetime and distribute the assets after you pass on. Here are some:

Avoid Probate

If you were to die after only preparing a Will to distribute assets upon your death, your estate MUST pass through probate, which is in itself a complicated and costly endeavor. The law says that before assets pass through a Will, the Will must be approved by a judge. *This is Probate.*

The entire probate process can take anywhere from a few months to a few years. This means that the Will's executor will likely need to hire an attorney to navigate the complexities of the court. Your trustee and beneficiaries must wait to access any assets that you had at death until the probate process is complete. This is an *expensive* and *lengthy* process. If you place your assets into a Lifetime Revocable Trust however, you avoid the probate process for those assets which you have placed into the Trust.

Consider the differences in the two scenarios:

1. John and Amanda are a couple in their late 40's, who own a home and have two teenage children. They wisely decide that they would engage in some estate planning. After a consultation with a qualified estate planning attorney, Wills are drafted for each of them, detailing their wishes of asset distribution when they pass away. Ten years later, within a few months of one another, both John and Amanda are diagnosed with terminal cancer. Each quickly deteriorates and they die one week apart. Their eldest child, now in their late twenties, calls the attorney who drafted the Wills and asks for guidance on how to distribute the property

and all accounts that both parents held at the time of their deaths. The answer is that BOTH Wills need to pass through probate, involving a lengthy and costly endeavor.

2.   John and Amanda decide that instead of solely preparing Wills for themselves, they take the advice of their estate planning attorney and use a Revocable Lifetime Trust and a "Pour-Over Will." They designate a successor trustee at the time of the Trust creation, who is a close friend. This trustee _does NOT necessarily have a vested interest in the distribution of the trust assets as a beneficiary, and has a role only to distribute the trust assets according to the terms of the Trust_. The couple's Pour-Over Will designates their Lifetime Revocable Trust as the beneficiary of their residual estate, which is everything they have, but which was not mentioned in the Trust.

Now, instead of a lengthy and expensive probate process, the successor trustee obtains a death certificate and brings it to a bank holding an account in the name of the Trust or brings it to an attorney to discuss selling the home to liquidate and distribute the Trust assets. Within weeks, and with minimal (if any) cost involved, the assets of the Trust are distributed to all of the beneficiaries of the Trust. This frees up estate assets to pay estate taxes, administration expenses and debts soon after their death.

It is EXTREMELY rare that the costs involved in distributing Trust assets exceed that of a probate proceeding. I have seen the difference in price of a probate/administration proceeding versus the distribution of assets held in a Trust to be in excess of $15,000.00. This number doesn't even begin to account for the reduction in the stress level of your loved ones at an emotionally difficult time.

The estate plan that utilizes the Lifetime Revocable Trust will be most efficient if all assets are titled in the name of the Trust. The Pour-Over Will serves as a catchall just in case you fail to take anything out of your name and place it into the Trust and also is logistically the document that may appoint the guardian who you choose for your children. The benefit is that by preparing this accompanying document, you can be assured that your assets (even those that might be outside of the Trust) will pass to the beneficiaries listed in your Trust in the way you determined. Note that since the Pour-Over Will is a type of Will document, it does need to pass through probate. However, assets that typically will pass through a Pour-Over Will are not likely to be major assets such as homes, large accounts, stock portfolios, etc. Most often, household belongings, jewelry, and small accounts are the property necessary to be distributed according to the Pour-Over Will, and most states (like New York) have created a specialized process to probate "small estates," which is typically a much more expedient and less expensive endeavor (by thousands of dollars) than a standard probate proceeding.

Planning for Disability

Another benefit in preparing a properly drafted Lifetime Revocable Trust is that it is arguably the best way to ensure that your property remains available to be used for your benefit, should you become physically or mentally incapable of managing your own affairs. While many people typically look to the drafting of Powers of Attorney (discussed later in this book) to accomplish this task, third parties such as banks, brokers and transfer agents often have more difficulty in dealing with a power of attorney than with a Trust. The reason for this is that, as a practical matter, financial institutions go to great lengths to train their employees about the pitfalls of honoring a non-valid power of attorney form. This is because the financial liability can be enormous if a bank or other financial employee mistakenly accepts an invalid document. Also, if the designated attorney-in-fact is unable to act, the power of attorney may not be usable. It is a much "cleaner" process to draft a Lifetime Revocable Trust and draft a defined order of those who you want to act in your stead in the event of a disability.

Note that if you become disabled and you have neither a revocable trust *nor* a power of attorney, an expensive, lengthy, and potentially embarrassing court proceeding is generally required to appoint a conservator or guardian before your property can be used to benefit either you or your family. Imagine a public court proceeding where your close family members are fighting over control of your assets while you are in a hospital bed. Even after a Guardian has been named, continued court supervision over the management of investments and disbursements is usually required. This can include annual bond fees, annual accounts and additional legal and accounting fees.

Now the question arises whether the preparation of a Lifetime Revocable Trust is an advisable option for young families. The answer is dependent on several factors; specifically the health of all family members and their general outlook on how prepared the family likes to be. If a young husband and wife visited my office tomorrow and explained that they were in good health and had two young children, I would explain to them the concept of using a Revocable Lifetime Trust, but I would certainly not insist on preparing one. Some practitioners operate this way and I feel this to be a short-sighted approach. Certainly, this type of Trust does provide a great level of protection against probate costs and disability issues, but my opinion has always been that the best estate plans are ones that grow over time along with a family. For a young family there is nothing wrong with starting with a standard Last Will and Testament and then revisiting the issues as the family ages and the dynamics develop. Common sense and statistics tell us that as people enter their 40s and 50s, different health problems begin to develop. Many people will, after consultation, decide to wait until they get into this age bracket to discuss the preparation of a Revocable Lifetime Trust. Others would rather prepare the documents as soon as possible, feeling secure that their family is using a well-drafted, advanced estate planning tool. Each individual family must make this decision, based on their own comfort level with each option.

Trust Type #2: Irrevocable Trusts

An Irrevocable Trust is, as the names suggests, a Trust that generally cannot be revoked. This means that once an Irrevocable Trust is created, the grantor loses *most* rights to modify the document and has absolutely no ownership over the assets named in the Trust. Contrast this with the Revocable Trust discussed previously, in which I said the grantor retains the right to use the account freely and typically includes an ATM/Debit Card and a check book. Another key distinction is that the Revocable Trust can be freely revoked or changed by the creator of the Trust; whereas an Irrevocable Trust cannot. Types of specific Irrevocable Trusts include Life Insurance Trusts, Charitable Trusts, Residence Trusts and Asset Protection Trusts. There are several other specific varieties and variations of Irrevocable Trusts, which a good estate planning attorney can explain, outlining the best option(s) to accomplish your long term goals. Like the Lifetime Revocable Trust, there are really two main, albeit different goals to be achieved by utilizing a properly executed Irrevocable Trust: reducing taxes and protecting assets.

Reducing Estate Taxes

While there is an entire chapter dedicated to estate taxes later in this book, they are worth mentioning here in the context of Irrevocable Trusts. Tax considerations are one of the prime reasons people create an Irrevocable Trust. Because a person relinquishes ownership of the assets named in the Irrevocable Trust, those assets are no longer part of the grantor's taxable estate at death. Later, I will explain why estate taxes are typically not of great concern to a young family. An added benefit to the grantor of these Trusts is that, in some situations, the income generated by assets is not taxed directly to the grantor. In many situations, an

Irrevocable Trust is considered its own tax entity with its own tax identification number. The taxes incurred by an irrevocable trust do, of course, have to be paid because the U.S. government would never allow income to accumulate tax free into the Trust. However, the difference is that the tax liabilities are managed by the trustee. Neither the grantor nor any beneficiaries are responsible for taxes incurred by the Irrevocable Trust

Asset Protection

The most common reason that I am asked to prepare Irrevocable Trusts is for asset protection purposes. Remember that the grantor no longer owns or receives benefits from any assets placed into an Irrevocable Trust. Therefore, *those assets cannot be seized by creditors*. Additionally, because they are not property of any beneficiary until the terms of the Trust distribute those assets, those assets cannot be claimed by any creditors of any beneficiary either. While the actual implementation of an Irrevocable Trust for asset protection purposes is not quite that simple and is subject to specific and lengthy rules, asset protection is available through the use of an Irrevocable Asset Protection Trust. For most of my clients who ask for an Asset Protection Trust, the concern is how to protect their assets in the event that they need to enter a nursing home or receive some kind of medical care, which would not be covered by their standard or supplemental health insurance. Common sense tells us that this is mainly a concern for people entering their golden years, and as this book is written specifically for young families, I will just mention the future availability of an Asset Protection Trust to protect assets from facility care costs.

As with a Revocable Trust, an Irrevocable Trust avoids the costly and time consuming process of probate. Remember that a court does not need to become involved with the distribution of assets when the division of assets has already been managed with a Trust.

Remember also that while Irrevocable Trusts can be very useful estate planning tools, as a general rule, the terms of these types of Trusts cannot readily be changed. Before executing this type of Trust, be certain to choose your beneficiaries carefully and cautiously consider which assets to include in this type of Trust with the help of your estate planning professional.

Chapter 4

Planning for Incapacity

Healthcare Directives and Durable Powers of Attorney

So far, I have discussed documents that anticipate the consequences of the passing of you or a member of your family. However, what if you are temporarily or permanently incapacitated? Life is not so simple as to exist only in the two absolutes of being a healthy and active member of society or being dead, so this becomes an important question to be addressed in the context of a well-drafted estate plan. There are several questions that become of the utmost importance:

Who will make medical decisions for you if you cannot do so yourself?

Who will handle your financial affairs for you and your children while you cannot?

In these situations, it is important for you to be prepared so that others can take care of your responsibilities while you are unable to do so. As part of a well-crafted and thorough estate plan, there are a series of documents that can be drafted so that others may handle your financial and healthcare decisions while you are incapacitated. These documents include but are not limited to: a Durable Power of Attorney (to make financial decisions); a Health Care Proxy (to make health care decisions); and a Living Will (sometimes called an "advanced directive"). Let's talk about each of these documents in detail.

Durable Power of Attorney

A durable power of attorney is a document through which you authorize a close family member or friend to engage in *financial* transactions on your behalf. If you become incapacitated, this document permits this person to handle your finances as if he or she were you. This authority includes the ability to pay your bills and file your tax returns, and could also allow him or her to use your finances to care for your children. Within the Durable Power of Attorney document, you can define the extent of the authority that you would like this person to have over your financial matters.

Without a power of attorney, your loved ones will not be able to gain access to your funds or make financial decisions on your behalf without first seeking court approval. Again, this is often a lengthy and expensive process. Even in situations where accounts are held jointly, there are situations where a spouse or other family member may not be able to gain immediate access to funds in an account. A power of attorney solves this issue. A power of attorney will allow the person you designated to manage, buy and sell your property if necessary, and to handle your insurance issues and government benefits if you become eligible for them. Essentially, the Durable Power of Attorney will allow for the person you choose to conduct all of your financial affairs just as if they were you. Be advised that there is a certain level of trust necessary to grant someone a

Durable Power of Attorney, because it does grant them access to your accounts and funds therein immediately. So, you must execute a power of attorney with a full understanding of its purpose, use and potential consequences.

Health Care Proxy

A Health Care Proxy is a document in which you authorize a close family member (often a spouse) or friend to make medical decisions on your behalf when you cannot. Without a Health Care Proxy (also called a "Health Care Power of Attorney"), all states have a default order in which your relatives will have the authority to make medical decisions for you. Because the law does not consider your personal family situation (a recurring theme in estate planning!), without a Health Care Proxy it is possible that you will have people who you do not trust or get along with making important healthcare decisions for you if you become incapacitated.

As an example, let's review the law as it currently exists in New York. All states have some similar orders delineated by statute. Since the 2010 passage of the Family Health Care Decision Act in New York, the law orders those making health care decisions as follows: (1) your guardian, if one has been appointed by the court; (2) your spouse; (3) adult children; (4) parents; (5) adult siblings; and (6) a close friend or more distant relative.

The preparation of a Health Care Proxy is important to everyone but it is VITALY important in the context of a family whose members have not officially been married. By executing a Health Care Proxy, in which you name a person and at least one alternate, you are able to override this default order. A prime example (and one that often arises) is if your spouse is also incapacitated or pre-deceases you . If you would prefer that your sibling make these type of decisions instead of your elderly parents, you can supersede your parents as decision-makers if you name your sibling in your Health Care Proxy document. Another great example is when a single parent becomes incapacitated and their children differ as to the care that the parent should be receiving.

Your health care agent's authority will only extend as far as was granted to them in the document. That being said, to cover the most important decision-making possibilities, this authority should include the power to access and disclose your medical records and other personal information; the power to hire and fire your doctors and other health care professionals; and the power to give or withhold consent to medical treatment. Basically, to be most effective, this person's authority should be that of your own as if you were able to exercise it.

Living Will

A Living Will (sometimes called an "Advance Directive") is a document where you can express your wishes about the level of treatment you would like to receive if you are found to be in one of three situations:

a)   You have a terminal condition;

b)   You are in a persistent vegetative state; or

c)   You have an end-stage condition.

The law defines each of these three conditions, and before a Living Will can be used, your doctors must certify that your situation falls into one of these three categories. In layman's terms and those that most understand, a Living Will is a document that explains your wishes about being kept alive on life support. The good news is that a well-drafted Living Will allows you to select which life sustaining measures you wish to utilize (if any). Several people wish to receive pain medication, for example, but not to be kept alive by a feeding tube or artificial hydration.

In a Living Will, you can leave directions to your Health Care Proxy and doctors regarding the level of treatment you would like to receive. From an emotional standpoint, memorializing how you would like a family member to act in a tragic situation is often invaluable, as it allows this family member to make difficult decisions with a clear understanding of your wishes. One final note about a Living Will: it is also a valuable tool to use in make specific directives as it pertains to organ donation.

The documents discussed in this chapter are equally, if not more important, than Will and Trust documents because you will still be alive when these documents are called into use. Think of the combined use of these documents as speaking for you when you cannot.

It is important to have frank and honest conversations about what your wishes are with your designated Power of Attorney agent and Health Care Proxy agent. If you feel that someone would be uncomfortable executing your wishes or would be unable to do so, then I strongly suggest you select someone who will be able to follow your instructions to the letter.

Chapter 5

Who Will Care For Your Children If You Are Unable To Do So?

I am often approached by clients, asking if they need to specifically designate a guardian for their children in the event of their incapacity. They fear that not doing so will make their kids wards of the state and place them in a foster home. The quick answer is: yes, you should designate a guardian for your children in the event you become incapacitated. But, if you don't, here's what is likely to occur.

The good news is that your child probably will not be made a ward of the state. The reality is that every state in the country has passed laws which require the court to select a guardian if you have failed to designate one prior to your death. Fortunately, the courts will usually seek to place your children in the care of a family member. The bad news is that "any person interested in the welfare" of your children may petition to become their guardian. The court obviously does not understand your family dynamics (and EVERY family has some dynamics). If multiple family members petition to become your children's guardian, the court may choose a different person to raise them than you would have chosen. In addition, it is possible that both sides of the child's family will petition to become the guardian of your children. If this happens, your children may end up in the middle of a lengthy and likely contentious court battle between their family members. Believe me when I tell you that there aren't enough adjectives to adequately express the horror of such a situation and the long term emotional trauma that a child can suffer as a result of it occurring.

You can save your children and your family a lot of heartache if, in your estate planning documents (specifically your Will or Revocable Living Trust documents), you and your spouse clearly indicate who you would want to raise your children should something happen to the both of you.

Some family members will not be receptive to the immense responsibility associated with the care of young children. I recommend having a frank conversation with your requested guardian prior to the drafting of your estate documents. Should they refuse to accept your wishes to be appointed as guardian, you could be back to that nightmare situation described above. It is with this in mind that I deem it vitally important to name a second guardian you would trust to raise your children in the event that your initial choice is unable or unwilling to do so.

Your requested guardian will essentially step into your shoes to make major parental decisions, such as how your children are to be educated, where they live and what medical care they receive. Therefore, it is important to pick someone who you think would make decisions similar to those you would make. Some questions that may help you determine your choice of guardian of your children are:

- Are they willing and able to serve as guardian for my children?
- Do they have the stability and ability to parent my children?
- Do they have the time and energy to take on the task of raising my children?
- Is their age or health of my designated guardian a consideration?
- Do they know and love my children?
- Do my children get along with them?
- Will they love my children and will they provide the support, comfort and nurturance that my children will need?
- Will they make it possible for my children to visit their grandparents, other relatives and close family friends?
- How far away do they live from family and friends?
- Do they have room for my children?
- Are their values and lifestyle comparable to mine?

- Will my children need to change schools and might they lose connections with friends?
- Do they share my religious beliefs?
- Do I trust them to make the best life decisions for my children?
- Would they raise my children in a substantially similar (or better) manner as I would?

One of the worst estate planning mistakes that you can make is to pass on without leaving specific instructions as to who you wish to care for your children. The small step of appointing a successor for your children's care is done as part of an overall estate plan in your Will or Trust document package, so there is really no extra work involved if you are having an estate plan prepared.

Chapter 6

How To Leave Property And Money To Your Children

Under the law of every state, minors cannot own property outright and, therefore, whatever you pass to your minor children upon your death must be managed by a "guardian of property." While in practice this is often the same person who I discussed in the previous chapter (the guardian of the person), it need not necessarily be so. Some people specifically will designate a different guardian of the property of a child to set up a sort of a "check and balance" type of situation.

Without any estate planning, the guardian of the property may have to post a bond and will be responsible for filing an accounting of your children's property with the court. This accounting can be a lengthy process and must be repeated each year until your each of your children reach 18 years of age. While one downside to this situation is that a court becomes involved in the upbringing of your child, the absolute biggest problem is what happens to your children's inheritance when they reach 18 years of age. Without planning to the contrary, the guardian of property is only permitted to maintain your children's property until they reach 18, at which point they are required to hand over complete control to your children. Thus, at 18 years old, your children will have unencumbered access to a potentially substantial amount of money without anyone to guide them in the management of their new-found wealth.

We say that it may be substantial wealth because their inheritance will include any life insurance proceeds they collect upon your death and any judgment awards from a successful claim that your estate may have pursued if your premature death was the result of some unlawful action.

As a general rule, it is unwise to give an 18 year old that much control over a large amount of property or money because it may lead to irresponsible spending. I have met plenty of 18 year-olds, who would likely be wise and responsible with any inheritance received. I have also met an equal amount of 18 year-olds who I wouldn't trust to be responsible with $100. The good news is that with the proper estate planning, you can protect your children's inheritance from both themselves and from others.

One option is to give your children's inheritance to them in trust (discussed previously in Chapter 3). Even if you are a complete neophyte when it comes to estate planning you have likely heard the term "trust fund," which is exactly what we are talking about here. You may be able to have your estate planning documents automatically set the trust up at your death so that the funds are not encumbered during your lifetime and they are available to you. By implementing this strategy, you can designate a trustee (discussed previously in Chapter 4) who you know and respect to manage your children's property without the necessity of court involvement. Furthermore, in the trust documents, you can guide this person on how to best use this property to provide for your children. If you leave your children's inheritance to them in trust, you can determine how old they must be before they are able to manage the property on their own You can keep the Trust in tact until your child reaches the age of 21, 25, 30, or 35 or any other age you decide. Also, an important and often unintended benefit of using a Trust for this purpose is that any property in trust for your children will not be accessible to any of their creditors for as long as they leave it in the Trust. This means that if they do become seriously in debt they can leave the funds in the trust and keep them protected from garnishment of any kind.

If you fail to set up a Trust to hold the inheritance for your children, along with the creditor and court involvement issues, you also will not be able to choose the person who will manage your assets for the benefit of your children. In some instances, a court may even appoint a complete stranger to dictate how YOUR money should be used to raise your children. As you can imagine, that situation can get very messy and it also happens very quickly.

Some young families prefer to include a provision directly in their Will, which would set some guidelines about setting up an inheritance trust following their death. Some states do allow this to be done directly within the confines of the Will. While this is an option and is one of the few exceptions as to when you can build a trust provision directly into a Will, the issues discussed in Chapter 3 will become a factor. As a refresher, such issues include probate and timely access to the funds. Note that in the next chapter, I will discuss some considerations if you have a Special Needs Child, which immediately brings many different and important issues into play.

By planning for the possibility that you and your spouse will die before your children are grown, you can continue to protect your children from themselves and from others, just as you would do if you were alive to guide them into adulthood.

Chapter 7

Planning For Special Needs Children

If you are the parent of a special needs child, there are additional precautions that you will need to take when preparing your estate plan. **Planning for Special Needs Children is always centered on preventing the inadvertent disqualification of children from public benefits that they would otherwise qualify for now or in the future**.

Many public benefit programs, such as **Medicaid**, require that a person applying for these benefits not have access to resources totaling over a very limited amount. If you die and leave assets to your special needs child in the same manner as your other children, you may disqualify your child for public benefits if, as a result, they could access resources over the limited amount. Please understand that this does not mean that you need to disinherit your special needs child. Most parents with special needs children are specifically sensitive to the issue of the long term care of their special needs child. Luckily, there are estate planning tools available that will allow you to leave assets to your child without the risk of disqualifying them for public benefits.

One popular tool that you may have heard of is referred to as a **Special Needs Trust (also known as a Supplemental Needs Trust**, which is basically the same thing). In its simplest terms, instead of passing assets outright to your child, this Trust restrict your child's access to the property just enough so that the assets in the Trust are not considered "available" to your special needs child for public benefit purposes. The Trust does not completely restrict your child's access to the Trust, but simply requires that the Trust be used only to "supplement" any public benefits he or she receives. When the special needs individual passes on, any money remaining in the trust will need to be used to reimburse the State

Medicaid Agency for payments made during the special needs individuals' lifetime.

The reason that this strategy is a great tool is that most often the State Medicaid agency will pay out FAR more money in public benefits over the course of the special needs individuals' lifetime than the amount that remains in the Trust at that same person's death. Of course, this planning strategy is completely legal and accepted by all public benefit programs (or I wouldn't be suggesting it here!)

Special Needs Trusts can provide benefits to and protect the assets of both physically and mentally disabled individuals. Another use of Special Needs Trusts are to hold personal injury settlement or litigation proceeds on behalf of a disabled person.

A Special Needs Trust for a disabled beneficiary may be set up in any state and even in many other countries that recognize the concept of the Trust. A common feature of Special Needs Trusts in all jurisdictions is that they may be run either by family members (a private trust) or by corporate trustees appointed by the court. More than in any other Trust, it is important that great care is taken to choose an appropriate trustee to manage the Trust assets and to deal with administering the Trust during the lifetime of the special needs individual and beyond.

One type of Trust that people often confuse with a Special Needs Trust is something called a "**Miller Trust**." The Miller trust is useful only in states which do NOT allow individuals to spend down any income above this level on their care until they reach the state's income standard. This type of trust is specifically used to qualify a Medicaid applicant with income in excess of the eligibility limit for long-term care (either facility or in-home) assistance from Medicaid. Such a Trust is technically not really a "special needs" trust as it will typically not be funded with the beneficiary's own assets (e.g. inheritance proceeds). In practice, The Miller trust is named as a recipient of the individual's income, from either a pension plan, Social Security, or other source. As with the Special Needs Trust discussed above, upon the death of the beneficiary, the State Medicaid agency must be paid back for its medical assistance from any remaining assets in the Miller Trust.

Another type of trust used for special needs individuals is something called a **Pooled Income Special Needs Trust**. Unlike the other trusts which are privately managed by private trustees, the Pooled Income Trust is run by a nonprofit association, and a separate special account is maintained for each individual beneficiary within the confines of the Trust. All accounts are pooled for investment and management purposes. The Trust (or more accurately, an account in the Pooled Trust) may be created by a parent, grandparent, guardian, or court, and it can also be created by the disabled individual. Upon the death of the disabled individual, the balance is either retained in the Trust for the nonprofit association or paid back to the State Medicaid agency for its medical assistance. While not of immediate concern for young families, it is worth mentioning in this discussion that in some states, a disabled individual over the age of 65 is entitled to transfer assets to a Pooled Trust and then be immediately eligible for Medicaid. In other states, the transfer must be made before the disabled individual attains the age of 66.

As you can well imagine, the complicated issues regarding the drafting of a Special Needs trust are aplenty and each situation will require some distinct insight and planning.

Chapter 8

What About Life Insurance?

Do I Need It And How Much Do I Need?

First, let me be perfectly clear that I am not a life insurance salesman. In my own opinion (although not shared by all), an attorney who sells life insurance has violated ethical rules regarding conflicts of interest. You should be aware that there is a lot of good information and a lot of misinformation floating around about life insurance. I hope to clarify the issue for you.

The question to ask yourself is: if you died tomorrow, would there be enough property in your estate to support your children until they are adults? For most of my clients, the answer to that question is a pretty solid "no." If you are among the fortunate minority who do have liquid assets right now that you think would cover the upbringing costs of a minor child, you absolutely need an estate plan to protect those assets for other reasons. Once you are gone, there will no longer be a paycheck each month to help support your children and therefore, what you have at this very moment will be what must provide for your children until they are adults. It is for this reason that now, as a young family, it is advisable for each family member to take out an insurance policy on their own life.

Before I delve into the need for life insurance and the options available to you in further detail, you should know that it's likely to be relatively inexpensive. There are two main types of life insurance available: term life insurance and whole life insurance.

Term Life Insurance

Term life insurance is written to provide a specific death benefit and protects an individual for a specific period of time in return for the policyholder's payment of a premium. If the insured person is alive at the end of the contract period, the premium is lost. In layman's terms, it's often thought of as a "pay as you go" type of insurance with no accumulation of money as you pay your premiums. It's as simple as this: you pay a premium every month and if something happens to you, the insurance company pays out your policy. There is a set term involved and you will often hear policies referred to as "10 year term life insurance" or "20 year term life insurance." You receive the benefit of being locked into guaranteed coverage for the term of the policy and the insurance company - through their actuaries (statisticians) – essentially bet on you surviving the term of the policy and not paying out on the policy. This is how they make (lots of) money.

It is important to note that that when the contract period extends beyond one year, the insurance company adds the individual mortality rate for each year and then calculates an average premium, which the policyholder must pay each year. The premium is the *same* during each year of coverage, priced higher than what the actual mortality risk would require in the earlier years, and less than the mortality risk in the late years would require.

Term insurance is particularly suitable to those purchasers who seek maximum coverage at the lowest possible cost for a specific period of time. Parents, for example, whose incomes are currently stretched to cover current living expenses, while trying to save for future liabilities (such as the college costs for children), may purchase term insurance until their children's education is complete. Term insurance is also ideal when a specific financial obligation will end at a certain future date, such as home mortgage payments. In terms of cost, the most recent available data (2015) suggests that the average cost of a 20 year term policy ($250,000.00) for a 30-35 year old non-smoker is about $27.00 per month. If you smoke you can expect to pay closer to $60.00 per month. The question that you need to ask yourself is whether $335.00 (non smoker) or $721.00 (smoker) per year is worth knowing that if something were to happen to you, your family would be entitled to a $250,000.00 check. You can, of course, take out $500,000.00, $1 million, $2 million or greater policy as well, but you will just have to be prepared to pay higher premiums.

A popular strategy in using term insurance is to take out a policy that reflects the number of years needed until your all of your children reach adulthood. If you have an infant and purchase a 20 year term policy, so long as you pay your premium each month, your death benefit will exist until your child is 20 or 21 years old; at which time, the child (who is now an adult) will theoretically be self-sufficient and not reliant on your finances for their care and well–being.

Whole Life Insurance

Also sometimes referred to as "**Permanent Insurance**," whole life insurance is simply an extended term insurance policy with an accumulating savings element. Like term insurance, so long as your premiums remain paid, the face value of the policy ($250,000.00 in my previous example) is paid to the beneficiaries upon the death of the insured. The difference is that your policy does not automatically expire at a certain term interval (10 years, 20 years, etc.) and part of your premium accumulates in the context of forced savings, which becomes available to you once a certain portion is paid into the policy. Basically, you pay premiums for the rest of your life, retain protection in the event of your death, but still accumulate savings that can be withdrawn (sometimes with penalty) or borrowed against. While whole life seems like a great idea (and for many people is), like everything else in life it comes with a cost. The monthly premiums for a whole life policy are higher. There may be some additional tax benefits available at your death with a whole life policy, but for most young families these aren't going to come into play at all. There are three major types of whole life or permanent life insurance—traditional whole life, universal life, and variable universal life, and there are variations within each type.

So which type of insurance is right for me?

For almost all of my estate planning clients who are young families the answer is term insurance. To borrow an insight that I was once told:

Think of whether you are protecting a risk of IF you die or WHEN you die.

For example, IF you die before the mortgage is paid off, then you want to have the insurance proceeds to pay it off. IF you die before the kids start college then you want to pay for tuition.

WHEN I die, my business needs to be sold. WHEN I die there will be estate taxes.

IFs are candidates for term insurance; WHENs are candidates for whole life.

In reality, it is never quite this simple, but I do think the "IF or WHEN" inquiry is a good place to start the analysis necessary when determining what type of policy is best for you and your family.

I've heard many financial planners discourage the purchase of whole life insurance, preferring to keep a client's savings and insurance elements separate. In my experience, a greater problem with whole life insurance (in the context of a young family) is that younger people starting a family and incurring significant long-term debts (e.g. mortgages) cannot afford the higher premiums, as the actual insurance coverage amount that they can afford for permanent (whole) insurance premiums is less than what is needed should they pass on with significant liabilities.

On the other hand, if you have a high income and problems saving money, whether due to a lack of discipline, time to manage investments, or knowledge about investment opportunities, whole life insurance may be perfect for you. The higher premiums of whole life include a forced savings element; the cash value of the policy will increase each year.

Another element to be considered is that whole life insurance might be ideal for people who have health issues or are worried that they might contract an illness that could lead to "un-insurability" as time goes by. A whole life policy can never be canceled (and doesn't expire) so long as the premiums are paid as required by the contract.

Regardless of the life insurance product that you purchase, the payout is likely to be a substantial amount of money. It is vitally important that you institute a plan for how your children will receive these benefits.

Just as with their inheritance (as discussed in Chapter 6), your minor children will not be able to own the proceeds from this life insurance policy. Without an estate plan, a court will put any payments made by the life insurance company to your children under the care of the guardian of property appointed by the court. Your children will receive, outright, the remaining proceeds at age 18, unprotected from creditors or their own irresponsible spending. Remember that as discussed in Chapter 6, a properly drafted estate plan can provide the necessary protection for your children to mitigate these concerns.

Chapter 9

Dealing With Retirement Plans In The Context Of An Estate Plan

Many individuals who are part of a young family will have some kind of retirement plan set up for them through their employer. At their core, retirement plans are created to provide investment vehicles for individuals so that after they have stopped working, they can retain the standard of living that they enjoyed during their working years. Accounts can be sponsored by an employer, as in the case of a 401(k) plan, or they can be Individual Retirement Accounts (IRAs). Most young families are operating under the umbrella of an employee-sponsored retirement plan such as a 401(k), and IRAs are usually reserved for those who own their own businesses or are typically set up once people enter their middle age years.

These retirement accounts are regulated by a litany of complex IRS (Internal Revenue Service) rules, which govern maximum yearly contributions, early withdrawal penalties, and mandatory distribution amounts based upon the age and life expectancy of the account holder. Let's first examine the three main types of retirement accounts and then we can analyze how they all work.

Pension Plans

Pensions are often called "defined benefit" plans because employees know just how much the plans will pay annually after retirement. Your employer sets aside some money each year that you work for the company, and a fund management company invests the retirement funds. Individual employees have little control over how the money is invested and often little information on what securities the pension is invested in. Employees generally receive a percentage of their ending salary once they retire. You may receive a higher percentage the more years you work, and your payout is typically not a function of how well the investments performed. Your employer may offer you an option to take a lump-sum rather than an annual pension payment. You may also be given an option of plans to invest in, with either aggressive or conservative options available. Pension payments are taxed as regular income once you retire.

IRA (Individual Retirement Account)

In IRA plans, employees make the contributions and these plans are owned and controlled entirely by the individual worker. Traditional IRA contributions may be tax deductible. There are defined yearly contribution limits in IRA plans and the individual is responsible for choosing which investments to make. The individual chooses how to invest the money and the return on those investments is uncertain due to market instability. There are additional restrictions on investing that need to be discussed with a financial professional. It is nearly impossible to estimate the value of your IRA when you retire. You can take as much out as you like each year after age 55 if you are retired. If you are still working, you may not take distributions until the year you reach age 59½, and the IRS will require you to take minimum distributions beginning at age 70½ for traditional IRAs, even if you haven't retired. You pay tax on traditional IRA distributions as regular income.

Roth IRA

Unlike Traditional IRAs, contributions to a Roth IRA are never tax-deductible. However, the money contributed to your Roth IRA can be withdrawn tax-free at any time. And, if qualified, an individual can withdraw the earnings tax-free, too. There are specific eligibility rules involved and not everyone can open a Roth IRA account. The amount you are permitted to contribute to a Roth IRA is limited to your earned income. Earned income includes wages and self-employment earnings, but does not include interest or dividends. If you are married, your combined contribution limit is restricted to the total of your combined earned income. For the year 2015, the most you can contribute to a Roth IRA is $5,500. If you have earned income, you can contribute to both a traditional IRA and a Roth IRA, but the combination of your contributions cannot exceed $5,500. Unlike in a traditional IRA, there is no tax deduction available for a Roth IRA contribution.

The real bread and butter of the Roth IRA is that the money that you contribute to your Roth IRA grows tax-free. You do not have to pay any taxes on the earnings in the account. In fact, you do not even report the income to the IRS. Even in retirement (when you ideally first access your Roth IRA money), you do not owe taxes on the distribution. If you take your Roth IRA money prior to retirement, it is likely that you will owe taxes on the distribution. Eligibility to contribute to a Roth IRA is restricted by your filing status and modified adjusted gross income. Keep in mind that the Roth IRA income limitations change each year.

The second really amazing benefit of a Roth IRA is that, unlike 401(k) plans and traditional IRAs (discussed above), there is no age at which you *must* begin to distribute money from your Roth IRA. As a result, Roth IRAs are an excellent tool to pass along wealth to your children or grandchildren.

Distribution Upon Death

When the owner of a retirement account dies, whether it be a 401(k), IRA, Roth IRA or other retirement plan, any amount remaining in the retirement account will pass to a previously designated beneficiary. The beneficiary is listed directly within the account, and so long as the beneficiary is alive at the death of the account holder, the money passes directly to the beneficiary without needing to pass through probate. It is thus vitally important to consider the amount that will pass to the account beneficiary when discussing the full distribution of all estate assets. A beneficiary can be any person or entity that the owner has chosen to receive the funds. It is also a good idea to name an alternate or successor beneficiary, who would take the funds if the originally designated beneficiary is deceased. The reason for this suggestion is that if no beneficiary is designated beforehand, the estate will generally become the recipient of the account, which as you know by now, will cause the account funds to pass through probate. If you decide to list your minor children to become either primary or alternate beneficiaries on the retirement account, be sure to list a guardian to manage the property until they reach adulthood.

The beneficiary does have some options in terms of what can be done with an inherited retirement account, but be aware that there are many tax consequences that come into play, depending on the desired option chosen. The IRS's broad array of rules and options are based on a few factors, which include:

a) Type of IRA (traditional or Roth)
b) Whether a beneficiary was properly designated
c) Whether the account holder died before or after the beginning date of "required minimum distributions" (RMDs - discussed later in this chapter)
d) Whether the account's sole beneficiary is a surviving spouse.

As they pertain to young families, the rules regarding taxation are really set up so that if someone in their 30's or 40's dies with a pension or 401(k) plan, the smart move is going to be keep the money tied up in either the original account or in a new retirement account until the money becomes necessary to maintain a standard of living. Through a discussion of all of the options available to a surviving family member, you will see why this is going to be the best option.

Options for a Surviving Spouse

A surviving spouse who is the *sole* beneficiary of a retirement account has a few choices. Here are their options.

Treat the IRA as their own.

A surviving spouse can elect to, essentially, just step into the existing account with the same rights and responsibilities of the deceased spouse. In this election, the same rules that applied to the deceased spouse will now apply to the surviving spouse. This means that the surviving spouse can then make contributions and withdrawals and name new beneficiaries as they see fit. The only differences when the surviving spouse elects to proceed this way is that:

a) Withdrawals are subject to a 10% federal income tax penalty if the spouse has not reached age 59 ½; and

b) The required minimum distributions begin at age 70 ½ of the surviving spouse.

When any funds are withdrawn or distributed from the account, all nondeductible amounts would be taxable as gross income. In addition, if required minimum distributions are not taken according to IRS rules, a 50% "excise tax" is levied on the amount that was not withdrawn, but should have been. (This penalty applies to *all* beneficiaries.)

Roll the account over into their retirement account.

Some retirement plans require that a deceased employee's account be distributed in a lump sum. In order to avert an immediate tax responsibility, which would normally accompany such a distribution, a surviving spouse could roll over the account into his or her own IRA or other retirement plan (or even create one if one doesn't exist). Surviving spouses have 60 days after the death to roll over the money. This is a smart idea when the family can maintain their current standard of living without the deceased spouse's retirement proceeds. Remember, the account will continue to grow as more money is placed into the account and the investment grows. As in the first option discussed, required minimum distributions would begin when the surviving spouse turns 70½.

Continue as the beneficiary.

This option works best for young families because the individual has died before reaching the age of 70½ and the surviving spouse has not reached 59½. A quirk in the IRS rules says that required distributions would be delayed until the point at which the deceased individual *would have had to make them. The surviving spouse would be able to withdraw funds without incurring the 10% early withdrawal penalty. Once the surviving spouse reaches age 59½, the account could be rolled over.*

A surviving spouse can also choose the "5-Year Rule" option because the spouse died before reaching the age of 70½. This election requires the surviving spouse to withdraw all of the funds by December 31 of the fifth year following the death. BUT, there are very tricky tax calculations to make when determining if this is the best available option.

So far, I've discussed what options are available to a surviving spouse of someone who has passed away. If a surviving spouse is *not* the sole beneficiary, different rules apply. In addition, there will be a different evaluation if the account is a Roth IRA or a similarly structured plan.

Options for Other Beneficiaries

When the beneficiary of a retirement plan is not the spouse of the decedent, different options are available. In general, this beneficiary has the following options.

a) To simply cash out the account and pay all necessary taxes on the distribution.

b) Take the 5-Year Rule payout option, if the account holder died before age 70½.
c) Treat the account as an *inherited IRA*, which would mean that minimum distributions need to be taken by December 31 of the year following the account owner's death.

Non-spouse beneficiaries cannot roll over an inherited IRA into their own account, nor can they treat the IRA as their own. In addition, non-spouse beneficiaries will likely be liable for paying estate taxes if the value of the retirement account plus other inherited assets exceeds estate tax exemptions.

Understanding the complexity of choices that face a retirement account beneficiary is key to satisfying IRS mandates, as well as maximizing the financial advantages of any inherited monies. Owners and future beneficiaries of retirement accounts are advised to seek professional advice before taking any action regarding them.

Chapter 10

Prenuptial and Postnuptial Agreements

Getting married is one of the biggest decisions that we all make in life. The love that you feel for a romantic partner is arguably one of the most enchanting experiences available to the human mind and heart. For most people, as their union approaches, the furthest thing on their minds is the idea that, at some point, there will be dissolution of the union. While the divorce rate nationwide has dropped since its peak in the late 1980's, it is worth mentioning that *someone gets divorced every 10-13 seconds in the United States.* I'd be willing to bet that over 99% of those marriages did not start with the parties believing that their marriage would end in divorce.

Contemporary marriage is, in short, an agreement involving your joined emotional and financial futures, and part of that concept is the shared ownership of property. This dual nature and purpose of marriage has led to the increased acknowledgment that a prenuptial or postnuptial agreement may be useful to protect each spouse's financial interests.

Prenuptial Agreements

A prenuptial agreement is a contractual decision made by each party as to how assets are to be distributed in the event that the marriage does not last until one spouse passes away. There is a certain stigma that accompanies the use of such an agreement. They are often viewed as uncaring, contractual documents that contradict the core values of being married in the first place. Many people consider the decision to use a prenuptial agreement as the decision to make a marriage practical instead of a romantic endeavor.

Instead of viewing a prenuptial agreement as some kind of cold, calculated document that immediately reduces the love that two people have for one another, it may be better to view the document as one that can actually bring harmony to a marriage by settling financial issues and keeping them from creating conflict during your life together and afterward.

If you can take a rational approach to your finances and disregard whatever stigma you believe is associated with a prenup, consider the invaluable benefits of having one in place. For those of any age, with any substantial assets, and/or children, a prenuptial agreement is strongly encouraged. Prenuptial agreements are particularly useful for people who are entering into a second marriage. In the case of remarriage, one or both spouses may already have significant assets and may want to make arrangements for family members from a previous marriage to inherit property and assets.

A prenuptial agreement is typically used to protect the assets that you have accumulated prior to your new marriage so that, for example, children from your previous marriage may inherit those assets. You can also use a prenup to have your new spouse waive rights as a beneficiary of your retirement plan. This is useful if, for example, you want your spouse and/or children from a previous marriage to be the beneficiaries instead. Your prenup can indicate that funds from a certain source (such as a business, stock portfolio, etc.) belong to one or both spouses, and in what proportions. The agreement can also indicate which debts are the responsibilities of one or both spouses, and in what proportions. The agreement can determine which of the spouses will manage business, investment, and banking details. And, of course, one spouse can make arrangements to distribute any type of assets to the other spouse.

Even if you are not entering into a remarriage, but you are bringing into your first marriage significant assets (and/or liabilities), a prenuptial arrangement might be a good idea. A prenup is also a good idea if the newly married couple has a large difference in age or financial status. The spouse with the majority of the assets will want to protect those assets and control their distribution, while the person with fewer assets will want to ensure receipt of some of the marital property in case the marriage ends due to divorce or death.

A prenuptial agreement is valid only if it is created under two conditions:

1. There must be "full disclosure" between the two parties, so that there will not be a finding of fraud, misrepresentation, or duress (a finding which would invalidate the prenuptial agreement). Both you and your spouse must thoroughly disclose your financial details: income, assets, and liabilities in the document; and

2. If attorneys are involved (suggested!) each spouse must individually be represented by *separate* attorneys prior to signing the prenuptial agreement; again, to reduce the risk of drafting and agreeing to an unfair agreement.

Once each of the conditions above are met, and the contents of the prenuptial agreement are satisfactory to both parties, you and your spouse each need to sign the prenuptial agreement before a notary. Be forewarned that creating an effective and fair prenuptial agreement requires a substantial amount of time and planning, so do not wait until immediately before the marriage to discuss and get to work on the agreement. Waiting until right before the wedding only increases the likelihood that the prenuptial agreement will be unsatisfactory to one or both spouses. It also increases the likelihood that one or both spouses will sign the prenuptial agreement under duress (potential cause for invalidation of the document).

An important thing to remember is that a prenuptial agreement is not just a document that protects and distributes assets in case of divorce. It is also a document that protects and distributes assets in case one of the spouses should die. Thus, the prenuptial agreement is not the exclusive tool of the divorce attorney, but is also used by the estate planning attorney on a regular basis.

Postnuptial Agreements

As with everything else in life, marriages change over time. Financial fortunes improve or decline, spouses develop new interests and habits, career paths diverge, and illness or death may change the marital landscape. Such changes can have dramatic effects on the status of the "marital estate," which is the property of the marriage. There is an estate planning tool that can be of immeasurable value during such mid-marriage shifts. The postnuptial agreement is that tool.

Like its counterpart - the prenuptial agreement - a postnuptial agreement is a contractual agreement between spouses regarding the distribution of property. However, while prenuptial agreements are executed *before* the marriage and are relatively common, post nuptial agreements are executed *during* the marriage and not currently as common. However, financially savvy couples are rapidly making the "postnup" a more popular vehicle for asset distribution.

Although couples in love may shy away from a prenuptial agreement, married couples tend to develop a clearer sense that marriage is about both emotional and economic health. Most people enter into a postnuptial agreement because the financial status of one or both of the spouses has changed significantly since the wedding day. As with the prenuptial argument, the purpose of the postnuptial agreement is to encourage a harmonious marriage, prevent future conflicts and build a stronger, more secure relationship and financial situation. Like a prenuptial agreement, the postnuptial can:

a) Determine the extent to which one or both spouses is the recipient of income from various sources;
b) Determine who is responsible for the debts from various sources;
c) Be used for a spousal waiver of benefits from a retirement account;
d) State the details of the division and/or distribution of property in case of divorce or death; and
e) Create harmony in a marriage.

Couples also enter into a postnuptial agreement because their goals and priorities have shifted during the marriage. Issues such as child care, household chores, investment decisions, and the like are often made part of the postnuptial agreement, either in response to (or in anticipation of) conflicts and changes of attitude in these areas. Still, while major changes in one or both spouse's financial status (either increased assets or increased liabilities) is a clear reason to create a postnuptial, the daily "nuts and bolts" of married life should not be neglected in such an agreement.

The same two conditions of the prenuptial agreement must be met with a postnuptial agreement in order for the document to be enforceable. As a reminder:

1. There must be "full disclosure" between the two parties, in order that there will not be a finding of fraud, misrepresentation, or duress. Both you and your spouse must thoroughly disclose your financial details: income, assets, and liabilities, in the document; and
2. If attorneys are involved (again suggested!)Each spouse must individually be represented by separate attorneys prior to signing the agreement, again to reduce the risk of drafting and agreeing to an unfair agreement.

In addition, each spouse must sign the postnuptial agreement and the agreement must be notarized.

Making an enforceable postnuptial agreement requires complete and truthful disclosure of all assets and liabilities by both spouses. A knowledgeable and experienced estate planning, matrimonial or family lawyer can guide you through the process of drafting a postnuptial agreement that works for you and your spouse.

Chapter 11

Handling Estate Planning Issues After A Divorce

Divorce statistics vary somewhat, but generally, newly married couples now have about a 45-50% chance of getting a divorce. Regardless as to how healthy a marital relationship is at the moment, it is an important part of my job, when setting up an estate plan for a young family, that I consider a future divorce of the couple. There are three important estate planning issues that need to be considered after a divorce or separation: Inheritance, Remarriage and Guardianship.

All are equally important, and each of these issues requires changes to any existing estate plan. For those couples with existing estate plans, many are under the mistaken assumption that the mere act of filing a complaint for divorce revokes all prior estate planning documents and beneficiary designations in favor of their soon-to-be former spouse. This is NOT true. If possible, a spouse should review and revise his or her estate plan and beneficiary designations before filing for divorce. In practice, it is most common that both spouses used the same attorney to prepare their estate plan. Due to a conflict of interest, it will be difficult for this same attorney to continue to represent either spouse when a divorce is imminent. Therefore, each spouse would be wise to seek a new attorney for estate planning purposes and should do so quickly once a divorce is contemplated. Once a complaint for divorce is filed, one spouse may seek an *ex parte* order[1] from the court prohibiting the other spouse from revising his or her estate plan documents and beneficiary designations.

Before and during the pendency of a divorce proceeding (as permitted by the court), Powers of Attorney and Health Care directive papers should be revised. They often designate one's spouse as agent and

---

[1] Ex parte means a unilateral communication to the court; one that need not be shared with the adversary, as is usually mandated.

authorized health care decision maker. Most people will not want their spouse to be in any position to make important financial or health care decisions (or most importantly, have access to their personal accounts) while the two parties are in the midst of a divorce proceeding. This is the case, even if the divorce is somewhat amicable. The mere filing for divorce likely does not revoke durable powers of attorney or a Health Care Proxy. Therefore, it is crucial to revise these documents and take affirmative acts, such as modifying/revoking these documents, notifying ALL institutions who may have a Power of Attorney or Health Care directive on file, and finally (after all necessary institutions have been notified), informing your spouse of the changes made. It is also important for both spouses to make sure that they update their beneficiary designations on any life insurance, retirement accounts, pay on death bank accounts, and investment accounts.

You may have noticed that I did NOT discuss making any changes to an existing Will or Trust. The reason for this is that ALL states have laws written that make it impermissible (to varying degrees) to disinherit your spouse. Even if you were to draft a Will, which clearly states that you want to leave ALL of your assets to your children and ZERO to your spouse, the law will permit your spouse to a specific proportional share of your estate.

The question then becomes whether a Will is invalidated by law once two spouses get divorced. The answer is both yes and no. Any provision of a Will executed by a married person that affects the spouse of that person becomes void upon divorce, dissolution or annulment of the marriage. After the dissolution, divorce, or annulment, upon the probate of the Will, the law treats the former spouse as if the former spouse had died at the time of the dissolution, divorce, or annulment of the marriage, unless the Will or the dissolution or divorce judgment expressly provides otherwise. So in short, a divorce does not invalidate the Will altogether but it does remove the spouse as beneficiary or Personal Representative.

Now let's turn to the specific issues involved in a divorce as they relate to children of the marriage.

Inheritance Issues

One major concern during a separation/divorce is what will happen to the inheritance of a child once a parent passes on. As discussed in previous chapters, the law and common sense tells us that a minor child will not be in any position to handle the complexities of handling an inheritance. Therefore, in most instances, a guardian is placed in charge of an inheritance.

Typically, when parents are divorced/separated and have a minor child, the guardian of both the person and property of the child will be the surviving ex-spouse. Many people have a big issue with this, as some marriages don't exactly end on the most amicable of terms. To prevent having your ex-spouse be in a position to manage the inheritance that you have earmarked for your child, we use what is called an **Inheritance Trust**. An Inheritance Trust is an irrevocable trust established through a deceased person's estate plan, typically for the benefit of a surviving child. Besides being able to select someone other than your ex-spouse as the trustee to manage your child's inheritance, the added benefit is that you can actually set the distribution to occur at any age of your child that you want. As we discussed in prior chapters, it is prudent to hold your child's inheritance until they reach an age where you can expect them to use their inheritance wisely. Until the child reaches the designated age, a third-party would be selected as trustee, who will have the responsibility of maintaining the trust and distributing the income and assets either to the guardian for the benefit of your child, or directly to vendors and service providers for the benefit of the minor child.

Remember that the trustee of an Inheritance Trust and your child's guardian will often be required to work together as the child ages. Therefore, be sure to avoid the designation of a trustee that conflicts with that of your ex-spouse. The best idea is for you and your ex-spouse to agree on someone with whom you both are comfortable to serve in this role.

Planning for the Possibility of Remarriage

We know that when most couples get married, their finances overlap, at least to some degree. The same is true for a subsequent marriage following divorce. So what happens if you fail to include provisions in your estate plan for your minor children from a previous marriage? It is possible that your new spouse could stand to inherit the majority of your estate, leaving a minor child without a share of your inheritance. This can be prevented by including some simple provisions in your estate documents or by setting up an Inheritance Trust as discussed above.

Guardianship Issues Following Divorce

Expounding on the issues above, as a general rule, if one parent passes away, guardianship automatically passes to the surviving biological parent, regardless of the status of custody, unless the surviving parent is determined to be unfit. What many people fail to realize, however, is the possibility that a minor child may need a non-parental guardian prior to reaching the age of maturity. This typically happens when the surviving parent also passes away prior to the child turning 18 years of age. This is another important reason to discuss guardianship issues with your ex-spouse. As is almost always the case in estate planning, if you can come to an agreement on this issue and memorialize it prior to the death of one ex-spouse, everyone can feel assured that the child will be taken care of properly, both physically and financially.

Once a divorce judgment is entered, all estate plan documents and beneficiary designations should be reviewed and updated to reflect the divorce. These are just some of the estate planning issues that may arise before, during and after a divorce. When divorce is imminent, a spouse should seek estate planning advice to accomplish his or her objectives.

Chapter 12

Estate Taxes and Gift Taxes:

What Is The Government Going To Take From My Estate?

Until now, most of the information contained in this book has been of the "tried and true" variety; meaning that the wisdom shared so far is universal for most states and is also typically unchanged by both federal and state legislatures. The topic of Estate Taxes is very different, however, with yearly changes and occasional complete overhauls of the methods in which estate taxes are calculated. Similar to how it works when you file your yearly income taxes, there will be two different tax entities who may request a portion of your estate at death, the federal government (IRS) and your individual state government.

The good news is that, for most people, and especially most young families, your estate will pass without owing any estate tax, meaning all of your money will go to your designated beneficiaries, without having to lose a slice in taxes. Estate and Gift Taxation is a very complicated subject, and as the purpose of this book is to introduce young families to estate planning concepts, my intent here in this chapter is just to introduce you to some basic tenets of the way that estates are taxed.

Federal Estate and Gift Taxes

For the majority of estates, whether a decedent is young or old, there will be no Estate Tax or Gift Tax due because under federal law you can bequeath a large amount of money and property tax free.

Federal estate and gift taxes are typically grouped together into something called the **Unified Gift and Estate Tax**. In 2016, you can leave or give away up to $5.45 million in total, before your beneficiaries need to pay a cent of federal estate tax. With such an exorbitant exemption amount on the books, you can see why estate taxes are typically not much of a concern to the average young family. This $5.45 million dollar personal estate tax exemption allows a property of almost any kind to pass tax free, regardless of who inherits it. The $5.45 million amount is indexed for inflation, so it will almost certainly increase in future years. If your estate is worth less than this amount - as are the estates of more than 99.5% of the population – you need not be concerned about federal estate tax. If you have made taxable gifts during your life (discussed later), the amount of your personal exemption will be reduced by the amount of those taxable gifts.

For those who are married, it gets even better! All property left to a surviving spouse - whether it is 1 million, 10 million or 100 million dollars - passes free of estate tax. One weird quirk of this rule is that the unlimited marital deduction is not permitted for property left to noncitizen spouses. However, the personal estate tax exemption ($5.45 million) can be used for property left to this small class of individuals.

Under IRS rules, a surviving spouse can also get a huge tax break when the time comes that they themselves pass on. If the first spouse to die didn't exhaust his or her individual tax exemption, the survivor can use what's left. *That gives the couple a total exemption of twice the individual exemption amount, which can be split between them in any way that provides the greatest tax benefit.* For illustration, say a woman dies and leaves $5 million to her widower. No estate tax is owed because property left to a spouse is tax-free. In the following year, the widower then dies, leaving $9 million (his own $4 million plus the $5 million he inherited from his wife) to their children. His estate won't owe any estate tax, even though the estate ($9 million) is over the exemption amount ($5.45 million) because the estate can use some of the husband's unused exemption.

All property of any amount left to a tax-exempt charity is also free of estate tax. This is why you see many ultra-wealthy people donating huge amounts of money to charity upon their death. Besides the noble philanthropic motivation behind leaving money or property to charity, many people would prefer that their money, which would otherwise go to the tax coffers, go directly to a charity of their choice.

As mentioned earlier, the federal gift tax is part of something that the IRS refers to as The Unified Gift and Estate Tax. The difference between a Gift Tax and an Estate Tax is that a Gift Tax refers to lifetime gifts, while Estate Tax applies to assets left at death. The two taxes are grouped together for IRS purposes so that the assets are taxed identically and at the same rate. This is why a dying multi-millionaire is not encouraged to avoid the estate tax by giving everything away just before death.

As previously mentioned, each of us can give away *$5.45 million in total* without owing federal gift and estate tax *either during our lifetime or after our death*. So, for example, if during your life you give your children your house, worth $500k, plus bequeath them another $4.5 million in cash and investments, no federal gift tax (or estate tax) will be due.

The same type of exclusion, which applies to an unlimited marital deduction also applies to gifts. Using the same scenario above, you can give your children the $500,000 house and $4.5 million dollars of other cash and investments, AND another $10 million to your spouse, and still not owe any gift tax.

If a gift is taxable, the person who makes the gift - not the recipient - must file a gift tax return. This is not like your federal yearly income tax return, however, as you don't file a return and mail in a check. Very few people end up paying gift tax at all during their lives. This is because a gift tax is not actually owed until a lifetime's worth of taxable gifts exceed the $5.45 million exemption. While we can all strive to have the wonderful problem of having to pay gift tax on gifts given over that amount, very few people give away that much money during their lives.

In short, at someone's death, federal estate tax is calculated. In addition to the property left behind (the estate), the amount of taxable lifetime gifts is included in the total that may be subject to estate tax. Again, no tax is due unless the taxable estate exceeds the exempt amount.

So what exactly constitutes a gift? In general terms, a gift is any transfer for which you receive nothing, or less than "fair market value," in return. For illustration, if you give your nephew a check for $1,000 because he graduated college, that would be considered a gift. Additionally, if you decide to sell your house, which is worth $500,000 on the market, to your son for $150,000, for gift tax purposes, you have made a $350,000 gift to him. In terms of calculating the fair market value of an asset, this would be the price at which an asset would sell when there's a willing and knowledgeable buyer and seller. As you can imagine, this is a tricky calculation. Anyone who has ever bought or sold anything knows that the value of something can only be calculated by looking at what someone has purchased that asset for. In real estate, this is an especially complicated analysis because the housing market is an ever-changing landscape.

Without even having to THINK about the gift tax, each of us can give as many gifts as we like during the year to as many different people that we want so long as each person is not gifted an amount that exceeds the annual exclusion amount of $14,000 (as of 2016). You can write a check for $14,000 to 2, 20, or 200 people every year and you will not have to pay any gift tax. Even better, you and your spouse can give $28,000 per year to each recipient.

There are other exclusions to what will be considered a gift for Gift Tax calculation purposes. The following items are NOT considered gifts for IRS purposes:

a) Tuition. But, only if you pay it directly to the school (Extraneous education expenses, such as housing, supplies, books and general living expenses, do not qualify for this exemption)

b) Medical expenses you pay directly

c) Gifts to your spouse (if your spouse is a U.S. citizen)

d) Gifts to a Political Organization (with exceptions)

e) Gifts to certain charities

In practice, if you make a gift that does not fall into one of the exclusions above (for example, you give your son $20,000 to help him pay for living expenses while he is away at college), then you'll need to file a gift tax return (IRS Form 709). *Remember that even though you file the gift tax return yearly when applicable, you don't pay the tax at that time. Instead, the amount of all non-exempt gifts made is calculated at your death and added to the inheritance that you are leaving to determine if any gift tax is due.* If at the time of your death, the non-exempt assets that you have and the non-exempt gifts that you have made in your lifetime total over the annual exclusion amount ($5.45 million in 2016), the amount over the exclusion amount will be taxed at a rate of 40%. If you are wealthy enough to be concerned about the federal gift and estate tax, you may end up hiring more than one professional adviser. It's common for an attorney to help a family craft an estate plan, while a CPA prepares tax returns and helps deal with the IRS.

One final note on Federal Estate Tax. There is something called the Generation Skipping Transfer Tax (GSTT). It is a complicated issue, but the basic concept of the GSTT is that it imposes a tax on both outright gifts and transfers in trust to or for the benefit of unrelated persons who are more than 37.5 years younger than the donor or to related persons more than one generation younger than the donor (such as grandchildren). The generation-skipping tax will be imposed only if the transfer avoids incurring a gift or estate tax at each generation level. The purpose of this tax is to close a loophole that existed wherein older people would just create a series of life estates that survived multiple generations, thus not being subject to federal estate tax. For example, property is placed in a trust for the donor's child and grandchildren. The income may be distributed among the child and grandchildren in accordance with their needs and the principal of the trust will be distributed outright to the grandchildren following the child's death. If the trust property is not subject to estate tax at the child's death, a generation-skipping tax will be imposed when the child dies. Again, the GSTT is an incredibly complex issue and subject to careful analysis, so be sure to discuss it with your attorney or accountant when planning your estate.

State Estate Tax

In addition to the federal estate tax, many U.S. states levy their own estate and inheritance taxes. While estate taxes are charged against the estate before distribution of the assets, inheritance taxes are something different. These taxes are levied on the transfer of assets to heirs, based on the specific relationship of the inheritor to the deceased. In the case of inheritance taxes, spouses, children, or siblings often have different exemptions. Unfortunately, every state has their own rules about estate and inheritance taxes so you may have to research your own state rules to get up-to-date information.

Currently, 15 states and the District of Columbia have an estate tax, and 6 states have an inheritance tax. For you unlucky residents of Maryland and New Jersey, your states are the super states, which charge *both* estate tax and inheritance tax. Lucky you. Again, keep in mind that this information is subject to change, as state legislatures love to play around with the estate and inheritance tax.

As of the date of publication of this book, the state with the highest maximum estate tax rate is Washington (20%), followed by 11 states which have a maximum rate of 16%; Hawaii and Delaware have the highest exemption threshold at $5,430,000 (matching the federal exemption). New Jersey has the lowest, only exempting estates up to $675,000. Of the 6 states with inheritance taxes, Nebraska has the highest top rate at 18%. Kentucky and New Jersey are close behind with top rates of 16%.

Reform and repeal of estate and inheritance taxes have been very frequent in the last few years, and it is a red-hot topic nationwide. In 2013, Indiana sped up the repeal of its inheritance tax, retroactively to January 1, 2013. Tennessee's estate tax will phase out fully in 2016. Maryland and New York are in the process of phasing in new, higher estate tax exemptions, eventually matching the federal exemption level ($5.9 million) by 2019. Minnesota is in the process of doubling its exemption from $1 million to $2 million over five years. The District of Columbia is slated to phase in higher exemptions to the estate tax as new revenues become available.

Credit Shelter Trusts

Earlier in this book, I discussed the use of trusts as a popular estate planning mechanism. Credit Shelter Trusts are another useful tool, although they are typically only necessary for those who are trying to avoid estate or inheritance tax issues in those states with low exclusion amounts. Credit shelter trusts are a way to take full advantage of state and federal estate tax exemptions. Although such trusts may appear needless unless you are a multi-millionaire, there are still reasons for those of more modest means to do this kind of planning. The main reason is state taxes.

As you now know, the first $5.45 million (in 2016) of an estate is exempt from federal estate taxes. Theoretically, therefore, a husband and wife would have no estate tax if their estate is less than $10.90 million. The estate tax is also "portable" between spouses. As previously discussed, this means that if the first spouse to die does not use all of his or her $5.45 million exemption, the estate of the surviving spouse may use it (provided the surviving spouse makes an "election" on the first spouse's estate tax return).

However, if one spouse dies and leaves everything to the surviving spouse, the surviving spouse may have an estate that is greater than $5.45 million, plus whatever is left over from the deceased spouse's exemption, or an estate that is higher than the applicable threshold in his or her state (assuming the state has an estate or inheritance tax). When the surviving spouse dies, any part of the estate over that threshold will be subject to estate tax. In other words, without proper planning, the exemption of the first spouse to die is lost. The way to preserve both spouses' exemptions is to create a "credit shelter trust" (also called an A/B or Bypass Trust).

Many states have an estate or inheritance tax and the thresholds are usually far lower than the current federal one. Let's say that a couple lives in State X, which has retained an estate tax on all estates over $1 million (this is the state's exemption). Looking at just the federal exemption of $5.45 million and the ability for the first spouse to die to transfer his or her unused credit to the other spouse, it would appear that the couple would have no tax issues if their estate is under $10.90 million. However, if the first spouse dies and passes everything to the surviving spouse, the surviving spouse may end up with an estate well over the state's

$1 million threshold and be subject to a substantial state tax upon their own death. In effect, the couple has lost the "unified credit" of the first spouse to pass away.

Standard estate tax planning is to split an estate that is over the prevailing state or federal exemption amount between spouses. Each spouse then executes a trust to "shelter" the first exemption amount in the estate of the first spouse to pass away. Although the terms of such trusts vary, they generally provide that the trust income will be paid to the surviving spouse and the trust principal will be available at the discretion of the trustee by the surviving spouse if needed. Since the surviving spouse does not control distributions of principal, the trust funds will not be included in her estate at her death and will not be subject to tax. This way, in State X, the couple can protect up to $2 million from estate taxation while still making the entire estate available to the surviving spouse if needed. Even if your state has no estate or inheritance tax, there are other reasons to have a credit shelter trust, many of which mirror the discussion above on the Lifetime Revocable Trust:

a) A Credit Shelter Trust shields funds in trust from creditors;

b) A Credit Shelter Trust protects children's inheritance if the surviving spouse remarries;

c) A Credit Shelter Trust helps avoid administrative headaches; and

d) In theory, we never know what Congress will do about the estate tax down the road.

It must be stressed that each state's disposition on estate and inheritance tax issues can change often; what is true now may be outdated next year. Therefore, be sure to consult with your attorney or CPA when making financial decisions based on state estate or inheritance taxes.

Chapter 13

Estate Planning for Unmarried Couples

New census data shows that the rate of unmarried people in a relationship who are co-habituating has doubled in the last 50 years. Unfortunately, as is often the case in many areas of law, Estate Planning laws nationwide have not fully been adjusted to reflect this statistic. A big reason for this jump is that the average life span increases every year. This means that more widows and widowers are meeting new romantic partners but do not get re-married. Another reason (and more appropriate for this book) is the fact that recent generations are not pressured to get married, as their parents and grandparents were, and simply don't want to be married or are persuaded to put it off until they're much older. Where gay couples are prohibited from marrying, co-habitation is their only means of legally expressing their commitment to one another.

Unlike the exemptions given to married couples discussed in previous chapters regarding estate taxes, unmarried couples cannot take advantage of these benefits. Without the legal marriage, any amount that passes at your death as part of your taxable estate will be subject to tax if it exceeds the annual exclusion amount. There is no grey area here; a legal marriage is required for these exclusions.

There are other estate planning benefits that are only available to married couples, such as Social Security payments, immigration status, joint bankruptcy filing and protection of spousal obligations, surviving spouse benefits, benefits under victim's compensation funds (e.g. 9/11 victims funds), and hospital visitation rights. While some states do recognize a form of "common law" marriage, the vast majority do not, and without additional planning, if one person dies, the remaining partner is not entitled to any benefits.

If you are living with a partner, who dies, you will not be entitled, by law, to any of the assets of your partner unless your partner has provided for you in an estate planning document. If your partner has suffered an illness or event, which lands them in the hospital, you may not be able to visit, as their family members are, and you will be unable to make any decisions for them. Legal devices such as a Last Will and Testament, Revocable Trust, Durable Power of Attorney, Health Care Proxy and Living Will enable you and your partner to provide for one another.

Keep in mind that all states have laws stating that one cannot disinherit a spouse. Yet, there is no state that has any law about disinheriting a life partner, mother, father, brother, sister or grandparent. A properly drafted Will or Lifetime Revocable Trust can solve the asset distribution issue.

Some other things to consider:

Life insurance.

Life insurance policies are another great way to avoid probating an estate and provide for your non-married partner. Be sure that you specifically designate your partner as the beneficiary of any life insurance policies that you own. You may also want to consider naming an alternate beneficiary in case your partner pre-deceases you. While that may not seem important now as a member of a young family, it is my experience that most people do not think to update their beneficiaries until it is too late. Setting up a primary and alternate beneficiary now can save you a lot of headache and heartache later.

Joint Tenancy

Joint tenancy is one type of co-ownership of property and for unmarried couples, it is without a doubt, the best option to protect your real property. Basically, joint tenants own property in equal, undivided interests. When one of the joint tenants dies, his or her share of the property passes directly to the surviving joint tenant. When you die, your partner inherits the home without probate administration.

Be aware that, even though joint tenancy avoids probate, property in joint tenancy (with rights of survivorship) doesn't automatically avoid estate tax. For unmarried couples, the value of property held jointly is included in the gross taxable estate of the first to die, unless the estate can prove the surviving partner contributed to the cost of the property. To prove the property wasn't a gift and verify your and your partner's shares of the ownership, keep accurate records of payments on jointly held property.

Employee Benefits

Similar to your life insurance policies, you are likely going to want to designate your partner as the beneficiary of your employer-sponsored retirement plan, such as pension or 401(k) plan. If your employer doesn't allow this, name your estate or trust as the beneficiary and name your partner as the beneficiary of your estate or trust.

Comprehensive estate planning is essential for unmarried couples. Careful planning ensures that you and your partner are included in important financial and medical decisions in the event one of you becomes seriously ill and that, on your death, your assets are transferred according to your wishes. Again, before making any estate planning changes, check with your state's estate tax laws. With the advent of same sex marriage laws, these rules are changing.

Chapter 14

Married and Unmarried Couples – Jointly Held Property

A dangerous misconception about Estate Planning concerns the belief that by virtue of owning property jointly with your significant other, estate planning is not needed. Holding assets, such as homes, cars and large accounts jointly does help mitigate the problems that can arise when one person dies. However, it does not eliminate the problems. As discussed, as a general rule, you should also designate each other as beneficiaries on any life insurance or retirement benefits.

Joint ownership itself is basically structured in three different ways and all will affect an estate differently. During the lifetime of each party to the joint ownership, all structures offer an undivided right to the use and enjoyment of the property. The ultimate consequences of how the property will be distributed at the death of one of the joint owners changes the rules of ownership of certain assets.

Joint Tenancy with Rights of Survivorship

In this arrangement, when one owner dies, full property ownership transfers to the surviving owner(s) through the built-in right of survivorship.

Tenancy by the Entirety

This is structured similarly to joint tenancy with rights of survivorship, except that it applies **only to married couples**, which would, of course, now include married same-sex couples in some states.

Tenancy in Common

Unlike joint tenancy with rights of survivorship, assets owned by tenants in common become part of the deceased owner's estate upon their death; therefore the property does not automatically pass to the joint owner. The decedent's share will pass through the probate (or administration) process in order for the property rights to be legally distributed.

Now let's discuss some issues that arise when people die while holding property jointly:

Remarriage

Especially when it comes to young couples, the likelihood that a spouse will remarry if one of them dies is quite high. If your assets are held jointly with your significant other, they will "inherit" those assets upon your death. Keep in mind that what happens to those assets, that is, your say in the matter, comes to an end upon your death. At that point, your partner can use or leave your property to whomever he or she wants. In the worst case, they can decide to leave it all to their new spouse, and this new spouse may decide to disinherit your children, leaving them without any inheritance from you or your spouse. Your spouse may have additional children with their new spouse and decide to leave part of your property to them. Or, your significant other may even decide to give it all away. In short, by holding everything jointly with your spouse, you risk unintentionally disinheriting your children, since you will no longer have control over where your assets should go upon your death. On the other hand, by using some of the tools we have already discussed, you can specify how you want the assets to be used during your partner's lifetime, and to whom you want the remainder of your assets to pass upon his or her death – e.g., your children. You can provide that your spouse should receive as much of the income and principal from your estate as he or she needs for health, education, maintenance, and support for life, but further specify that the assets will be distributed to your children upon your spouse's death.

Avoiding Probate or Estate Administration

If you were to die today without having done any estate planning, your estate would be subject to an Administration Proceeding in the Surrogate's Court. There, the court would supervise the inventory and distribution of your liquid and non-liquid assets to your beneficiaries under a standard set of laws known as the intestacy laws of New York State. The state will determine who will receive the proceeds of your estate and in what share. A common misconception is that if you die without any estate planning documents that all of your money will go to the government. In actual practice it is very unlikely that this will happen, because even people who don't have close family, most likely have some traceable sibling, niece, nephew, cousin, etc. who would be entitled to the estate proceeds.

There is also a trend developing nationwide where courts are beginning to look carefully into joint accounts when one party to the account dies. In the past there almost seemed to be a "carte blanche' type of rule available to those who pass money via joint accounts at their death.

Now, some courts are now actually reviewing account histories to see if the account was a true joint account or simply an account set up as a method to bypass the probate/administration system, what is commonly called an "account of convenience." Holding accounts jointly is not enough. The cost to properly prepare the necessary documents is almost always less than the cost of an attorney to handle the probate or administration proceeding or other headaches associated with the joint account.

Chapter 15

Social Media Accounts and Digital Assets

As we move further every day into a digital age, more and more people will need to begin to plan for the disposition upon their death of "digital assets" and social media accounts.

Digital assets are things like files, electronic mail, digital documents, audible content, motion picture content and other media and even the devices, which contain these items, like computers and other storage devices. Photographs, illustrations, documents and anything else you can think of that can be placed onto an electronic drive are assets, which belong to you. If you own a business, if you are an artist or if you have valuable contracts on your computer, these are your assets, which need to be protected from improper distribution upon your death.

So the question then becomes: What will happen to these assets if I become disabled or when I die? Would a family member know where to find important documents The answer to this question should be contained in a proper estate plan.

Social Media Accounts

You may not have taken stock in just how much information and visual media you have stored within all of your social media site accounts. Much of the information stored on computers and all of the information stored on an online e-mail or social media account is password protected. Unless you make arrangements in advance, how can you expect a family member to be able to access these? You risk losing the information stored digitally forever if you fail to prepare for this event. Estate planning for digital assets and social media accounts is similar to estate planning for other assets. First, you should make an inventory of what you have, name someone to step in for you when the time comes, provide that person with access, and provide some direction for what you want to happen to these assets. Here are some good tips to get you started on this.

Make a Physical List

Make a Physical (printed) list of your digital assets and accounts and keep it with other important Estate Planning Documents. Listing these by category will help make the task less daunting. Categories might include:

Hardware: Include computers (laptop, desktop, work computer), hard drives, off-site backup service information, usb flash drives, tablets, cell phones and cameras (which might have digital photos stored in them).

Include a general overview of where they are located and what is on each one.

Software: At the least, this would include important word processing (MS Word i.e.) and spreadsheet (MS Excel i.e.) documents; Quicken or

Quickbooks for financial records; tax preparation programs and past tax returns.

Social Media and Online Presence: Facebook, Instagram, Vine, Twitter, LinkedIn, Flickr, YouTube, Snapchat, your own website, your blog, online backup sites, online sites on which you store photos and/or work documents.

Online Accounts: Bank and other financial accounts; email accounts and very importantly Amazon, other shopping sites and bills that you pay online may have your credit card or bank information stored on them.

Designate a Successor

Think about who you would want to access your computer, your email, and your online accounts in your absence. This person will need to have some computer know-how. It may be the perfect job for the teenager or young adult in your family, or you might have a good friend who could help. It would be a good idea to talk to this person now and let others know your plans. It is also prudent to select only one person to handle this responsibility, but picking a successor individual is a good idea also.

Provide Access

Next to each account, be sure to list user names, passwords, PIN numbers and the website address (if applicable). If you change your password, you'll need to change it on the list. While we are cautioned to never write these down, it will be necessary for your successor to have them in order to gain access. Keep this list in a safe place (I recommend a small fireproof safe that can be purchased at any office supply or big box store) and tell your successor where it is. Common sense tells us that this document should be a hard copy and not be stored on your computer. Computers crash and get stolen and you would be defeating the whole purpose of the exercise if your successor cannot access your computer.

Provide Instructions

Facebook, LinkedIn, Instagram, Twitter, websites, blogs and email accounts can all be used to notify others of a death. Facebook will "memorialize" a user's account so that others can view it and write remembrances on the user's Wall. Email can be configured to send an auto-response informing the sender of a death and where to forward information.

If you want a site to continue if you have a website or blog, you need to leave instructions for keeping it up or having someone take it over and continue it. If there are things on your computer or hard drive that you want to pass on (scanned family photos, ancestry research, a book you have been writing, etc.), put them in a **"Do Not Delete"** folder and include it on your inventory list.

Closing down accounts that are no longer needed will help to protect your family from identity theft after you are gone. If you want an account to be closed, you may want a copy made and saved first, especially if it contains photos or writings.

Estate Planning for digital assets could have extraordinary and unforeseen consequences. There is the story of Pewdiepie (pronounced Pew- Dee – Pie), a 26 year-old Swedish man who started a YouTube account in 2010 and began making videos of himself playing video games. As of 2015, his net worth was estimated to be $42.5 million, just from recording himself playing video games. That YouTube account is probably worth tens of millions of dollars, and is of course an asset, to be distributed at his death. If you think that his story is an isolated incident, it's not. In every genre and interest group there is now a person or group of people who are making absurd amounts of money as the supposed "authority" in their area on YouTube and other social media sites. And more sites are coming in the future. It will be fascinating to see how technology further advances us as a society in terms of communication and entertainment, but one thing for certain is that as digital issues grow, so will the need to include them in a properly drafted Estate Plan.

Chapter 16

Pets and Pet Trusts

As someone who grew up in a household, which, for the most part, didn't include pets, it took me by surprise the first few times that I met clients who had very real and serious concerns about the welfare of their pets after their death. What I quickly learned is that for many people, pets are as important to them as any other family member. With this important concern in mind, I will tell you how you can make provisions for the care, maintenance and support of pets after your death.

Leona Helmsley was a successful and renowned hotel owner and real estate investor who died in 2007 at age 87. Wisely, and in accordance with the same advice that I give to my clients and the readers of this book, she left no ambiguity about the distribution of her more than **$4 billion** estate. Helmsley created a 14-page Will (it was filed in the New York County Surrogate's Court and can be found online fairly easily), which specifically allocated her assets. Most of her assets were given to the Leona M. and Harry B. Helmsley Charitable Trust, which continues to this day to engage in worthwhile charitable contributions. What is most interesting about her Will, however, is that she designated $12 million of her assets to a trust for the care of her beloved 8-year-old white Maltese, Trouble. (She made separate provisions about the care of the dog itself, who she entrusted to the care of her brother). From 2007 until his death in 2011, there was a dog in New York City who technically had a net worth of millions of dollars.

You can certainly provide adequately for your pets by creating a Pet Trust.

Pet Trusts

Like any other Trust, Pet trusts are created and used during the pet owner's life. The benefit here is that the trust survives the death of the pet owner. A key point to be made is that owners can be assured that their pets will be cared for should the owner become incapacitated or ill. Pet Trusts can also be carried out immediately upon death or disability because owners determine when the Trust becomes effective. You can specify whether it get triggered if you get sick, if you die, or under any other delineated circumstances..

There are really two issues to consider when creating a Pet Trust:

Who will care for the pet and be the pet's guardian?

Who will pay for caring for the pet?

You need to trust your pet's guardian because it's pretty easy to defraud a dog or cat. How would your pet ever be able to let anyone know that the money wasn't being used for their care and support? There can be safeguards included in the Trust to help decrease the possibility of anyone using the money set aside for your pet for their own personal use. You can also be very specific about how often any funds should be dispersed, what happens if the pet has offspring, and precisely how you want your pet cared for. Considering your pet's probable lifespan, you can also specify in the Trust how you want any remainder balance distributed.

If you have considered your pet in a Will, keep in mind that a pet trust is not a complicated document. Also, a Will only takes on any legal effect in terms of property distribution after death. Therefore, your Will cannot address the care of your pets during your lifetime. Another reason why Wills are not a great option for this purpose is that there is usually a waiting period between the death of the pet owner and the time when the Will actually is filed and probated. Here, the issue is not simply distributing money and property. A pet is a living creature, requiring immediate attendance; it cannot afford to go months without receiving care. Most importantly, if you use only a Will, there is nothing that prevents someone from using the funds intended for the pets for their own benefit.

Chapter 17

Estate Planning for the Same-Sex Couple

If you are a person who is involved in a same-sex relationship, it is likely that you have heard of the historic Supreme Court decision from June, 2015 in the case of, **Obergefell v. Hodges**. In short, the U.S. Supreme Court in this case affirmed a constitutional right to same-sex marriage in all 50 states, opening up tax, estate planning and employee benefits opportunities for couples in the 13 states that had not previously permitted same-sex marriage.

Before **Obergefell**, same-sex couples in these hold-out states had to make estate planning decisions based on a set of laws that was in flux.

Between the differences that existed in various states about the legality of same-sex marriage and the constant state court decisions speaking on the matter, it was a confusing landscape even for someone well versed in following such situations. It seems that after Obergefell, there is no turning back on the issue of same-sex marriage. Married same-sex couples must now by law receive the same rights and benefits of any other married couple. Let's examine some key issues.

Income taxes

With respect to income taxes while alive, married same-sex couples can now file joint federal AND state income tax returns, which typically leads to a lower tax liability than filing two individual returns. Remember, because of the federalism concepts of the 10th Amendment to the Bill of Rights, states retained rights not specifically reserved to the federal government. Before Obergefell this led to an amazingly frustrating situation, where many people were permitted to file their federal income tax return jointly but had to file their state tax return separately. Now same-sex married couples can file both their state and federal tax returns jointly.

Gifting

As we discussed earlier in Chapter 11, a big advantage of married status is that you can make unlimited gifts to your spouse without worrying about federal or state gift taxes. This will help same-sex couples who have been stuck with federal gift tax bills when they've bought a house. Now if a same-sex couple buys a house together, even if they put in different amounts towards the purchase price, they can have joint 50-50 ownership of the house with no gift tax consequences.

Estate Planning and Estate Taxes

We also talked in previous chapters about the spousal exclusion that allows spouses to leave one another property without paying estate taxes at the first death. **Obergefell** extends that spousal exclusion right at all levels to same-sex couples. Equally if not more important is that married same-sex couples can now claim the spousal election on any estate. For a quick refresher, the spousal election is a law on the books in all 50 states that states that you cannot disinherit your spouse and that by law a surviving spouse is entitled to a specific percentage of a deceased spouse's estate.

Health Care Directives

By now you know that if you are not planning to prepare a Health Care Proxy and Living Will that you are, in the opinion of this author, missing the boat. For same – sex couples, the post **Obergefell** difference for health care directive purposes is that the same-sex spouse does step into the role of a traditional spouse, which comes into play when someone has not designated any proxy or Living Will agent. Remember that as it pertains to same-sex spouses, this does NOT mean that you should forego the preparation of healthcare directives, as the same issues discussed in Chapter 3 of this book still apply.

For those involved in a same-sex relationship that are not married, your rights have not been changed by **Obergefell** and your rights remain in line with those involved in a traditional heterosexual relationship. You can still receive inheritance through a will, and be named as a Health Care Proxy and Durable Power of Attorney. The problems arise in both a traditional and same-sex relationship when those involved in the relationship choose NOT to get married (and thus entitle them to the specific benefits enumerated herein) OR prepare any estate plan.

Chapter 18

Legacy Planning

So far, I have discussed various mechanisms to passing on money and property to your family. This chapter deals with the non-physical, legacy-related issues of your estate plan and how to pass them on to future generations. When we think of our families and the next generations of our family, we want those memories to be positive and vibrant. That is why, if we want to leave a meaningful legacy and have our lives be about more than the assets that we leave to our family members, we must have a plan. Legacy Planning is defined differently by different practitioners, and the term is often grouped together with an overarching estate plan under one umbrella. I disagree with this approach and feel that it is important to separate the financial implications of the passing of a life from the emotional and value-based things that will survive us all.

You need not be wealthy or famous to have a Legacy Plan. A legacy is the transfer of family values, goals, dreams, and history, which every family has. Every family has a history that should be shared with future generations. Every family also has goals, dreams and aspirations for future generations. A current trend in estate planning is for people to draft a personalized letter and include it in their estate planning materials for their relatives to find after their death. Many people refer to this as a "family love letter." Consider the profound emotional impact that a personalized letter may have on a loved one. Also consider the fact that even future generations not yet born can read a family history that pre-dates them and know what the core values and dreams of their ancestors were. This letter also goes by another name - an **Ethical Will**, but this is a term that I don't like to use because it has unintended connotations.

A smart attorney can help facilitate conversations that can memorialize the client's wishes, values, life experiences and lessons learned. He or she can help the client articulate what is truly important and what they would like to share with friends and loved ones. The conversations can be recorded for future reference when reducing the client's thoughts to writing and they can be edited into a final visual or audio representation of the legacy letter if the client desires. Some issues that I will discuss with my clients in creating their legacy plan are the following:

• Thoughts on money and wealth

• Personal keepsakes and treasured heirlooms

• Wisdom to be passed to children and younger family members

• Thoughts on work/life balance and life success

• Core values and life lessons learned

• Thoughts on religious and spiritual beliefs

• Thoughts on love and relationships

- Regrets and life opportunities not taken

- Memories, anecdotes and specific stories

A final issue to consider when determining how to craft your legacy involves the use of charity. Is there a cause that is close to your heart? Have you always felt a special connection to a specific philanthropic group? Even if just for just a nominal amount such as $100 or $1,000, planning to leave money to a charity is a great final statement to your family as to what you hold dear.

Legacy planning is also something that is fluid. Just as classic estate planning is something that is usually done and revisited periodically to ensure that it still reflects the wishes of the individual, for many of my clients, legacy planning is an ongoing project. Many create folders and files where they keep treasured documents, articles, awards, newspaper clippings, notes, greeting cards, and anything and everything else that may reflect their life message.

Chapter 19

Estate Planning for Family Business Owners

Due to the explosion of the internet and other technology devices, more people today operate small businesses than ever before. Many people own and operate small businesses as a part time job and use the proceeds as monthly supplemental income. As with everything else that you own, ownership of a business interest of any kind is something that needs to be addressed within the context of a well-crafted estate plan.

By creating a detailed estate plan for your family business now, you can be secure knowing the company will transition smoothly when you're no longer around. There are some key things to prepare for now that will make the eventual succession as painless as possible.

Ownership Transfer

After a family business owner passes on, those left behind are often left scrambling to make decisions about who should be doing what portion of the necessary work. A good business estate plan doesn't just address ownership transfer, but can also help coordinate the day-to-day management and operations of the company after the owner's death.

I counsel my clients to make sure that their estate plan includes details on dealing with everyone involved in the operation of the business, including corporate members, consultants, employees, associates and shareholders. It is also important to determine how to address the business's key employees. Additionally, it's important to specify who will be running the business if this person is different from the individual who ends up owning it. Taking the above steps before a death will help protect the business for years to come.

If you're the sole owner of your family business, you can create an estate plan that details the transfer of ownership and managerial power to your next of kin, just as you would transfer any other type of property that you own. The situation becomes more complicated for family businesses with multiple owners. In these cases, it is imperative that the company bylaws or shareholders agreements outlines a specific plan to deal with this situation. Not only should these documents dictate who can and cannot acquire shares after a current owner passes on, but it may also prevent spouses and children from becoming owners by requiring surviving shareholders to buy out the deceased member's portion of the business.

Tax Considerations

Typically, for those who own and operate small businesses, a majority of their wealth is going to be intertwined in many ways with the business operations. It is therefore imperative to take steps to protect your loved ones from unnecessary tax payments when you're gone. Without an estate plan, your business's new owner may be on the hook for a hefty estate tax. Few family businesses possess enough cash on hand to cover the tax burden. New owners will have to make the terrible choice between selling the company and taking out large loans to cover the tax burden.

One of the benefits of estate planning is that it lets family businesses plan for the future and take advantage of applicable IRS tax breaks. There are tons of ways for a business owner to get creative in structuring the company and distributing the assets. For example, a business owner may want to gift stock to family members during his or her lifetime. While doing this prevents the owner from having to pay income tax on the gift, family members may be on the hook should they decide to sell the stocks at a later date. Business owners may also want to consider a stock's short and long-term tax situation before gifting it to younger family members.

Documents used for Succession Planning

Detailed legal documents are crucial for protecting your family business after a death. Earlier, using a Revocable Living Trust to transfer assets at death was discussed. For a business owner, this is an ideal route to take because you can transfer your business interests directly into the Trust. The Trust then effectively owns your ownership share in the business but still allows you to continue to make all decisions. As a reminder, assets included in a living trust, like your business, will not be subject to normal probate-related proceedings after death. Additionally, a living trust assists family businesses in transferring ownership. After transferring the company to the trust, the owner can specify a successor right in the trust document. This person will take over the Trust at a designated time, usually upon the owner's death or disability. Forming a living trust can also reduce estate taxes that would apply during the probate process.

While a living trust is ideal for single-owner businesses, companies with multiple owners (e.g. partnerships, multiple-member LLCs, corporations) may require what is called a *buy-sell agreement* to protect their assets. Also known as buyout agreements, these documents prevent beneficiaries from being burdened with businesses they don't want, while protecting partners in the event of one owner's death. By using a conservative valuation formula when creating the buy-sell agreement, owners can lawfully establish the value of the ownership interest at a price beneath the sales value upon death.

An estate plan doesn't just protect your family, it also safeguards the legacy of the business you worked hard to build. Business owners can arrange for the transfer of a company during their lifetimes, thereby minimizing the chance of the family either losing the business or being subject to a loss on a sale of the business. Like in all other aspects of estate planning, establishing a plan now while you're still around, enables you to enjoy running your business while secure in the knowledge that your family business is in good hands.

Chapter 20

Making Changes:

How Your Estate Plan Should Evolve As You Age

If you have read, digested and are ready to take action based on what you have read so far in this book, then you are well on your way to attaining the peace of mind that comes with creating a strong estate plan. Although your estate plan is concrete, life evolves. Therefore, your estate plan must be modified as your life changes.

After you've crafted your initial estate plan, your circumstances are likely to change. You may have more children, acquire more assets, change your marital status, or experience a change in your relationships with those who you've named as beneficiaries. These and other life events may require changes to your estate plan. I am not advocating the re-drafting of any estate planning documents every few months or even every few years. What I do advise is that you review the plan every five years or so, just to make sure that what you wanted a five years ago remains what you want today. Ask your practitioner to prepare a breakdown of all beneficiaries and bequests. It's a good idea to review your Will and/or Trust documents along with your inventory of assets and list of beneficiaries every five years or so to make sure your past decisions continue to meet your current needs. Do not think of estate planning as a one-time transaction, but as a process that works best if periodically reviewed.

How do I change my Will after it has been executed?

You can change your Will any time before you die. You can add assets, beneficiaries or revoke bequests, so long as you are physically and mentally competent to make the change <u>and</u> employ the proper formalities. You can change your Will entirely – throw it away and make a new one – or just tweak it. An amendment to a Will is called a codicil. It is executed with the same formalities of a regular Will but doesn't require rewriting the entire Will again. Tt is merely attached as a supplement to your original document.

NEVER attempt to manually make changes to the estate planning documents yourself. It will become unenforceable. You can't strike out a clause and write another one in its place. Any changes, amendments or supplements to estate planning documents must be executed using the same procedures that were used when you executed the original documents themselves.

Besides the periodic review suggested above, there are some situations, which would cause me to recommend a review of your estate planning documents. Some examples include the purchase of a new home, divorce or remarriage, moving to another state, substantial increase or decrease of income, birth of children, death of relatives, and all other major life or financial changes.

When and how should I revoke my Will entirely?

There are situations where it is easier and more beneficial to just create a new Will, as opposed to amending or adding to an existing Will with a codicil. Major life changes might warrant a total overhaul of your Will, which means scrapping the old one and starting fresh with a new one. Once you create a new Will, the old automatically becomes void. Keep in mind that if your new Will cannot be located at the time of your death, but the old one wasn't destroyed and is available, the old Will becomes enforceable. If it's the only document around, which expresses your wishes, then it's the one that will be used to determine distribution of your assets. So, make sure that you set your old Will on fire once you create a new Will (or just shred it …).

What happens if I fail to keep my Will up-to-date?

Some life changes may be accommodated by the law, regardless of what your Will provides. For example, if you have a new child and don't explicitly say you don't want him or her to inherit anything, the law will give the child his or her legal share of your estate. Likewise, a new spouse will be entitled to inherit a portion of your estate even if you fail to specifically name him or her in your estate plan. Moreover, if you come into property that is not accounted for by the Will, it becomes part of your residuary estate; it will pass to the person or institution designated to get everything not specifically identified in the Will. The problem with relying on the statutory distribution rules is that you run the risk of paying higher taxes, bequeathing property to people you may not intend to, or creating confusion (and possibly probate delays or even litigation) among your relatives after you're gone.

What about amending a Trust?

You can make changes to certain types of trusts, and those changes are called amendments. You should amend your Trust when you want to change or add beneficiaries, take assets from the Trust or change trustees. You don't have to write a formal amendment to the Trust to add property to it since a properly drafted Trust will contain language giving you the right to include properly acquired after the Trust is drafted.

As with a Will, you should revoke, not amend, your trust when making major changes. You revoke a Trust by destroying all copies of it or writing "revoked" on each page and signing them (or setting it on fire). Before you go ahead and destroy the document, make sure that anything you place into the Trust is removed from it. When you create a new Trust to replace a revoked one, give the new Trust a different name, usually one containing the date the new document was executed. Unlike Wills, Trusts have names.

Estate planning is part of your life. Your life is ever-changing, so make sure that your estate planning changes accordingly.

Chapter 21

Advanced Planning Techniques

Up until now, I have outlined a set of tools that many young families can use to give themselves peace of mind to protect their families. In this chapter, I want to introduce you to some advanced planning concepts that are much more likely to become considerations as you get older and begin to more strongly consider the precise distribution of your estate upon your death. All of the tools discussed here are advanced trust mechanisms, which are all carefully crafted to accomplish a specific purpose. Most of these specific trusts deal with the elimination of Estate Tax issues. As discussed previously, the IRS allows you to pass on assets totaling 5.45 million dollars without paying federal estate taxes. Yet, for most young families, these advanced techniques are not utilized. A general understanding of their uses and benefits can prepare for when you get older or if the estate and/or gift tax exemptions should ever change.

Irrevocable Living (Bypass) Trust

This type of trust is a way to give ownership of an asset without giving the recipient unencumbered access to the money or property. If you relinquish all rights to income and principal from the Trust, as well as the power to change the Trust agreement in any manner, the asset will not be part of your taxable estate. As with all other trusts, you list the beneficiaries of the Trust, including both income and principal beneficiaries. Because the initial transfer is considered a gift to the Trust, a gift tax may be imposed unless the transfer qualifies for the annual or lifetime gift tax exclusion (discussed previously in chapter 12).

Irrevocable Life Insurance Trust (ILIT)

The ILIT combines two tried-and-true estate planning mechanisms: the Trust and the life insurance policy. Basically, you set up an Irrevocable Trust, which itself owns the life insurance policies on your life. This then removes the proceeds of such policies from your taxable estate (and potentially keeps your estate under all federal and state estate tax exemption amounts). If not done this way, your life insurance proceeds become part of your estate. The added benefit of using an ILIT is that it offers a tremendous amount of immediate flexibility to accomplish estate objectives. Unlike property and even investment accounts, which must be liquidated, insurance policy payouts are made by check. This money may then be used to buy non-liquid assets from the estate or loan money to the estate, thereby eliminating any need for distress sales of estate property or excessive borrowing which might be needed to pay estate taxes.

An irrevocable life insurance trust should be used when it is desirable to remove life insurance proceeds from the taxable estate and effect the management of the death benefit proceeds. Those with larger estates and those with closely held businesses, real estate or other non-liquid assets, should seriously consider using these trusts in almost all cases in which they wish to obtain life insurance. If transfers of existing employer-sponsored and personal policies are made to an irrevocable trust, the insured must survive the transfer by 3 years for the policy proceeds to avoid estate taxation. Gift taxes on payments of premiums may also have to be paid if the Trust is not properly drafted (as technically you may be considered to be making a gift to your trust to pay the premiums).

A common objective of an ILIT is to minimize any gift tax consequences on payment of premiums and on the transfer of life insurance policies to trust. For new policies, the trustee should be the applicant, owner and beneficiary of the new policy. In either situation, cash gifts are generally made to the Trust by the policy donor. The trustee then pays the insurance premiums due.

If it is an estate planning objective to transfer existing policies out of the taxable estate of the insured, the insured must give up all "incidents of ownership" in the policies. This means that the person who gives up the policy must not retain control over the use of the policy in any way (e.g., the right to name a beneficiary or to borrow against the policy). Transferring the insurance to your spouse will not accomplish transfer tax savings because the death benefit would become part of your spouse's estate. You must transfer such policies to your children or other beneficiaries or to irrevocable trusts for their benefit and/or the benefit of your spouse.

To sum up, the Irrevocable Life Insurance Trust can provide income for your heirs; avoid probate; reduce estate settlement expenses; prevent life insurance proceeds from being included in your estate; and provide funds to pay estate taxes and other estate settlement costs at deeply discounted rates.

Qualified Personal Residence Trust (QPRT)

This Trust allows you to transfer your residence or vacation property to a trustee on a highly leveraged transfer tax basis, while continuing to use the property for the term of the Trust. The QPRT is often used to "freeze" the value of estate assets for estate tax purposes. This is a complicated type of trust and I urge you to speak with an estate planning professional to fully understand the IRS tax basis rules of property ownership.

Grantor Retained Annuity Trust (GRAT)

A Grantor Retained Annuity Trust is another estate freeze technique. The grantor creates an irrevocable trust and transfers assets to the Trust in exchange for an annuity payable over a term of years. To the extent the Trust assets grow at a rate greater than the IRS Section 7520 rate, the excess is transferred to the beneficiaries free of estate and gift tax at the end of the trust term. This is another complicated type of trust and estate planning mechanism that really must be discussed with an estate planning professional.

Asset Protection Trust

In addition to protecting your assets while doing Medicaid planning, a general Asset Protection Trust also allows you to protect your assets from the claims of future creditors. Asset protection is important to individuals who own businesses and is especially important to those who have high-risk professions, such as doctors, where there is a threat of medical malpractice lawsuits. People with asset protection concerns want to ensure, at all times, that their personal assets and business assets are always kept separate, and that they are insulated from cross-liability between the two. Traditionally, if you place assets into a Trust that you create and receive some benefits from, the assets in the Trust are not protected from the claims of creditors. However, some states, such as Delaware, have laws that allow self-settled trusts to be protected from creditors in certain cases.

Dynasty Trust

A Dynasty Trust can be established to pass your assets to your children, grandchildren and great-grandchildren, while protecting the money from creditors. It also allows the funds in the Trust to avoid estate taxes at the death of your child, and again at the death of your grandchildren, allowing the funds to grow without tax liability, thereby aiding the transfer of wealth from one generation to the next. Unfortunately, the only states permitting the use of a Dynasty Trust are Delaware, Nevada, South Dakota and Alaska.

Chapter 21

How To Select An Estate Planning Attorney

Now that you have a basic understanding of what you may need, an important next step is to find out who can best prepare an estate plan that is perfect for you.

Estate Planning (aka Trusts and Estates) Law is a multi-dimensional and complicated field that is in a constant state of flux. New laws and regulations are continually enacted by federal and state legislatures. Every decision released by a court or administrative body represents a new interpretation of legal concepts, making the waters even muddier.

Many attorneys in private practice may choose to limit their practice to certain areas of the law. Others prefer to manage a "general practice", where you can get a consultation for a divorce case and a criminal case from the same attorney, in the same office, on the same day. In smaller communities many attorneys find it necessary to engage in this type of "general practice" to serve a wide range of clients. Other attorneys however, especially in a more urban area, may focus their practice on a particular field of law, which for our purposes for this discussion would logically be estate planning, probate and trust administration. This does not necessarily mean that any one type of attorney is "smarter" than another, but rather is illustrated just for purposes of this discussion.

Some people already have a relationship with an attorney that they have done business with in the past. In many instances this was a real estate attorney who helped a young family purchase their first home. If you have a good rapport with any attorney who may have worked with in the past it is a good idea to contact that attorney first for guidance. Even if that attorney does not engage in any Estate Planning, he or she will always be able to refer you to a colleague that does. What I have learned is that attorneys with similar personalities and skill sets tend to gravitate towards one another, so if you had a pleasant experience with an attorney it is likely that you will enjoy working with his or her trusted colleague.

Another great idea is to ask trusted friends and family for referrals. In this respect this is no different than if you needed an exterminator, a tree trimming service or a pediatrician for your child. In particular, think of someone who you may know who has recently gone through the estate planning process, which might include family members, friends or other professionals with whom we are acquainted. Ask others, "Have you had a will or trust prepared? Who did that work for you? Would you recommend that person to others?" Start to assemble a list of the names that you receive and prepare to make some initial contacts.

Next you should research the recommended attorneys online to see if they are licensed in your jurisdiction and also to see if they have received positive reviews. As with all online reviews it is important to take anything you read with a grain of salt but I would be wary of an attorney who had a litany of bad reviews online. This likely speaks to either an issue in competence or communication with his or her clients. Once you decide on your top choice to consult with call the office and explain that you are interested in having some estate planning done and that you would like to schedule an initial consultation with the attorney who has been recommended to you. Always ask up front what the fee will be for such an initial meeting. The reality is that some attorneys offer free initial consultations and some charge a fee for the time spent meeting with prospective clients. One thing that others may advise you to do which I do NOT advise is for you to make several appointments with different attorneys at once and spend a week going from office to office. I think this is EXTREMELY shortsighted, as this technique will only serve to leave you confused and overwhelmed by the end of the week. Instead, you should meet with one attorney, digest the information received, and then decide if you would like to then speak with another. Then repeat that process until you find someone that you would like to work with.

It is vitally important to arrive at any meeting with an attorney prepared to explain your circumstances and perhaps even what kind of work you may need done. It is a good idea to provide a rough sketch of any accounts, assets and liabilities that you have. It is also possible that the law firm may have an estate planning questionnaire.

During an initial consultation, you should have some questions prepared to ask the attorney. These questions are intended to assist you in getting to know the attorney and that individual's background in estate planning. Some good questions to ask may be:

1. For how long have you been an attorney?

2. What other types of law do you practice other than Estate Planning?

3. Do you participate in yearly continuing legal education in the field of estate planning to ensure that you are up to date with current developments?

4. How else do you keep up with changes in estate planning law?

5. Will anyone else in the office be working on my file, and if so, can I meet them?

6. Can you give me an estimate of how many estate plans you have drafted in the past 12 months?

7. If my estate plan includes a trust, will you assist in transferring assets into the trust? Is that included in the fees or are there additional fees?

8. What exactly will be included in my estate plan?

9. Can you give me an estimate of how long the estate planning process will take and approximately how many meetings you anticipate us having during the entire process?

12. What is your opinion of how often an estate plan should be reviewed?

You should not feel awkward or uncomfortable about having such a conversation with the attorney. The estate planning process involves personal decisions about valuable lifetime assets. Believe me, all attorneys are well aware that your comfort in the process is paramount to your decision making in who to hire as an attorney. Be inquisitive but not disrespectful or condescending. Contrary to popular belief, as a general rule attorneys *do* like to work with well-informed clients. It saves time in explaining things (sometimes many times over) and can create a real symbiotic relationship between attorney and client. This is what you are striving for.

One final note on selecting an attorney. In Estate Planning, as in everything else in life, you do truly get what you pay for. I strongly urge you not to "price shop" and just select the attorney with the lowest fee. This isn't a big screen TV that we are talking about, this is a real investment in your family's future. You will be far better served to choose the attorney who you connect with and who you feel will do the right job, regardless as to whether that attorney is not the cheapest available option.

Chapter 22

Summing it all up

It is my sincerest hope that you will now seriously consider making an estate plan for your future and the future of your family. It's an important thing to do. As you now know, it doesn't need to take much time or effort; and even some basic planning will create a lifetime of security for you and your family. Everybody makes plans for their future, but the rub of life is that we very rarely can know for certain what the future will hold. Estate planning is an exception however, because it plans for the inevitable. I can guarantee that you will at some point pass on, and that anything that you own will need to be distributed at your death. Estate Planning is a real investment in your family's future. Unlike other investments however, the likelihood of a successful return on investment (peace of mind during your life and an easy process for your family to deal with when you pass) is essentially guaranteed.

By now you know that this book is about money, asset and procedure planning for when you die or become disabled. But, at its core is also about compassion and love. It about the love you feel toward others and the love they feel toward you. This is why you need to plan and that is why you read this book: for those you love. Never lose sight of that.

Appendix

There are a myriad of resources available online to further read about any of the topics discussed in this book. Please remember however that you should always ensure that you are researching your own state-specific information, as there are certain planning strategies available in some jurisdictions that are not applicable in others. Here are some of my favorite websites which can help de-mystify some of the more confusing sub-topics of Estate Planning.

EstatePlanning.com

AmericanBar.org

Investopedia.com

Nolo.com

NerdWallet.com

Kiplinger.com

ElderLawAnswers.com

Last but not least, if you took the time to purchase and read this book, I want you to have my personal e-mail address - matt@lenzalawfirm.com.

The law restricts me from giving you legal advice and please don't e-mail me with your specific story or issue, but if you are confused about a specific topic covered in this book I may be able to point you to additional resources that may be of help.

Made in the USA
Middletown, DE
27 September 2016